Sacred Awakening

Poems, Essays & Illustrations

CHRIS AHRENDS

This is a gentle book. A book packed with wisdom and searing honesty, a book to be savoured. A word of caution as you come to these quiet pages, just know that you will be transformed.

The Revd Mpho Tutu van Furth

With integrity, authentic solidarity and a compassionate passion for change Chris sees the lived-reality of others. In a spirit of true allyship, he offers poems, stories and reflections on contemporary social justice issues, deftly woven into contextual theology and social activism. This contribution, steeped in a profoundly caring spirituality, captures the wealth of Chris' experience and work as priest, pastor and poet.

Dr Miranda Pillay

Chris Ahrends has consistently been a thought leader in drawing the church to look with deeper compassion at God's world and to contribute more significantly to a liberated and freedom-loving society. He always draws attention to the need for a firmer grasp on matters related to greater security for the most vulnerable amongst us. He is a true example of living a Jesus-driven life.

The Revd Canon Courtney Sampson

Visualising a place and time when all are accepted and none experience discrimination is a sacred and holy task. In this anthology, Chris offers us a holy moment ... and has given us words that awaken this vision.

Bishop Vicentia R. Kgabe

Through story, prophetic poetry and courageous reflection, Sacred Awakening is a visionary call beckoning the female heart beating and breathing in each of us to open a new portal into experiencing church that is warm and welcoming – relational and always open – to all.

Dr. Judith Mayotte

In this beautiful book of essays and poetry, Chris' life-themes of peace and justice, church and the world, feminist spirituality, and engaged humanism receive the tender treatment that few can give with Chris' conviction. At a time of so much violence, and with the COVID-19 pandemic so central to our human life and conversations, Chris is to be congratulated for giving this nation much food for thought.

The Revd Canon Dr Barney Pityana

I found a number of pieces in this remarkable anthology/memoir by Chris Ahrends, priest, pastor, therapist and pilgrim, heart-breaking, reducing me to tears. Chris gives himself permission to be vulnerable and brutally honest. We, the readers are witnesses to an intimate conversation Chris is having with himself on his pilgrimage to becoming his true self in our land suffused with unremitting pain. Chris courageously tells us who he is and some of what he has learnt so far. His writing provides a mirror and invitation to the reader to introspect and own who we are. … The degree to which Chris is able to give words to his own deepest feelings as he also compassionately accompanies others will touch the hidden recesses of many hearts.

The Revd Michael Lapsley SSM

Copyright © 2021 by Chris Ahrends. All rights reserved. No part of this publication may be reproduced, distributed, or transmitted in any form or by any means, including photocopying, recording, or other electronic or mechanical methods, without the prior written permission of the publisher, except in the case of brief quotations embodied in reviews and certain other non-commercial uses permitted by copyright law.

First published in South Africa in November 2021 by Chris Ahrends
Ashley Cottage, 7 Upper Quarterdeck Road, Kalk Bay 7975,
Western Cape, South Africa

ISBN: 978-0-620-97090-7

Printed by Print on Demand, Cape Town, South Africa

TRIGGER WARNING
Some sections in this book contain poems and reflections on violent crime, gender-based violence, explicit language and accounts of trauma, which may trigger strong emotions and/or memories of violence-related trauma. If you need help, please do not hesitate to reach out to a counsellor or agency offering trauma counselling. There is no shame in asking for help. We are not islands. We need each other. Reach out and find help, or maybe reach out to someone waiting for you to listen to their story.

Contents

Introduction — 8

The Future is Female — 10
Allyship in the new age that's coming

This Curséd Violence — 33
Turning desolation into gentle chimes of meaning

Did God Give Me This? — 73
Finding a home in the land of otherness

The Broken Teeth of Failure — 94
Endings are new beginnings

Spiritual not Religious — 117
Communities as wombs of awakening

Journeying in the Desert of Love — 166
Trust your heart – it knows the way

Sadhu, May I Walk With You? — 203
Embracing the path of emptiness

Lee's Farewell — 233

A Final Word — 239

■ ■ ■

**Dedicated to
LEE RICHARD COLTHAM
(26 July 1974 – 30 August 2021)**

■ ■ ■

The breeze at dawn has secrets to tell you.
Don't go back to sleep …

RUMI

Becoming is hard work.
Staying the same is even harder.

TITILOPE SONUGA

Introduction

Although this anthology is titled *Sacred Awakening*, in no part have I addressed 'awakening' as something we all experience or need to encounter. Nor do I believe I have 'awoken'. This isn't a self-help book. It doesn't suggest that by taking particular steps or following particular lessons you will awaken. But, it is an anthology of poems and essays suggesting that 'awakening' is possible – that we can live *wakeful* lives.

Many of the poems were written during the seven years I spent, largely, among the beautiful people of St Margaret's Anglican Church in Parow, Cape Town. These were my final years of full-time parish ministry, during which time I came to see more clearly that before us, as the human family, lay several cataclysmic challenges – each of which impacts not only our collective or communal lives, but also our personal lives.

The challenges include, in my view, the patriarchy, the trauma of violence, our inability to face failure, and the increasing atrophy of our social organisations – in my case, the organisation to which I had given much of my professional life: the church. I should have added to this list our gross and crass exploitation of our planet. However, living in the midst of these seemingly insurmountable challenges, I stumbled upon what I sensed was some form of medicine: insights that could help, heal or open a new way of being in the world.

Advancing the girl-child, embracing rituals of lamentation, entering into profound processes of personal and organisational self-reflection, practicing meditation, and embracing communal and personal self-emptying, are all practices that will bring us closer to an awakening, to a new and inclusive consciousness, to that 'garden', as Rumi described it, in which there is a place and enough for all.

This anthology brings these writings and illustrations together in one humble and fallible manuscript. I've tried to illustrate several of the poems – and am deeply grateful to have had the time this year to attend an inspirational weekly art class, during which most of the illustrations were created.

Are the chapters really lessons? Do the lessons work? Is there a path that leads us to an awakened future? Do these writings offer any clues? I don't know.

But what I *do* know is that there is a garden, 'beyond right and wrong', and it's big enough for all.

Let's meet there?

Chris Ahrends
"Ashley Cottage"
Kalk Bay, South Africa
December 2021

The Future is Female

Allyship in the new age that's coming

■ ■ ■

'DO YOU SEE that little girl over there? In this state [Kerala], if she wants to become a doctor one day, she'll be given all the assistance she needs. Her brother, however, will have to compete like everyone else.'

We had stopped at a dhaba *– a roadside café – on the way to the Kurisumala Ashram high in the tea-plantation hills of Kerala, one of the 28 states of India. Our taxi driver explained that, for many years, the Kerala state government had placed the girl-child at the heart of public policy and planning. With almost 35 million inhabitants, Kerala has been the most progressive state in India for several decades. Years of policy reforms and affirmative planning actions in Kerala have brought about the lowest poverty rates, the lowest infant mortality rates, and the highest literacy rates in the country (for example, literacy among women in Kerala is 88%, while in India generally it is 54%), among other pleasing statistics.*

There are more health clinics per capita, more schools, and so on. The point is that advantaging the girl-child has raised the welfare of the entire state.

The future is female! Wouldn't this be amazing? Imagine 10,000 years of 'the age of women' replacing the past 10,000 years of patriarchy that have brought us to the edge of yet another extinction; this one, the sixth, called the Holocene extinction, in which we ourselves are the matter of extinction!

We need a different future: one that starts by placing the girl-child at the centre of everything. The age of patriarchy and its culture of toxic masculinity must end. Over hundreds of generations – and in many different forms, cultures, religions, empires and communities – the patriarchy has mastered the art of domination, exploitation and manipulation. Supremacy has always been the goal; ownership, desire and violence the means to the end. The resulting suffering continues today and women largely pay the price.

The energy needed in the world today is not the extroverted masculine energy of power and control, of problem-solving and domination, but the introverted, subtle energy of immanence, of presence – an energy characterised by enquiry, understanding, intuition and inclusion. This energy is feminine and women are its primary custodians. And I seek allyship with this liberating energy and the women committed to bringing it into the world.

Some will say that what I'm really looking for is 'a feminine future' and not 'a future that is female'. But no, what I'm wanting *is* a female future. It won't be enough to simply try to make the patriarchy more feminine. It would be like the apartheid apologists who suggested apartheid could be reformed. It couldn't. It had to be replaced with a completely new order. We need a female future – one that begins with making the girl-child the central building block – for at least one-hundred years. We need a revolutionary replacement of the patriarchy in every sphere of life. Everyone, including men, can participate in the creation of this new reality.

In Celebration of Grandma

Mary the model *Grandma*

Let us awaken to, celebrate and hold onto the inherent strength of women, especially those who have shown us how to stand firm over many generations. It is this essential strength that will empower the required and revolutionary birthing of our preferred future. I've experienced this sublime strength in many women, but never more than in the lives and love of mothers, *gogos* and grandmas…

In Celebration of Grandma

Grandma's heart was a vast and gracious place
for me to hide and heal;
me, her last born *laaitjie*
the-one-she-loved-more-than-the-others
which were, she'd say,
a 'ghastly horde'
though she loved us all without condition.

Grandma's face was like the ever-dawning morning sun
to be explored and enjoyed
rising each day, over endless steaming pots to feed us all
her flour-flecked cheeks aglow, her *doek* a
sparkling crown upon a regal brow
frowning just enough for you to know
her mind was more agile than our sleepy cat,
her arthritic knees notwithstanding.

Grandma's silver hair was brushed each day
before the bedroom mirror that hung
all the years by a silver chain from the picture rail;
I often watched her from under the *kwilt*
of her warm and welcome bed
into which I crept
when a scary dream had frightened me;

but never did she sit, I often thought, for long enough
to see the braids of beauty
gazing back at her,
so visible to me even at a tender age.

Grandma's hands were like *kastrolle*, scrubbed with soap,
yet tender to the touch,
like when she heard my cry
and never questioned why I wet my bed, but instead
with those broad warm hands
would guide me to her room
and hold me close enough to smell
the forest lingering there, all pine and free,
from when just she and me,
went picking mushrooms
about which she knew more than anyone.

Grandma's body, was an immense *naghemel*,
an overarching firmament
filled with stars of light; and once,
her bathroom door, ajar just a little, as I passed,
and not knowing to look away
I saw her naked, from behind,
putting on her dressing gown,
and from that day, each time I touched
her fiery frame, glowing all saffron-brown
I felt deep down, that I too was a star of light.

Grandma's eyes were like kites, soaring through the sky;
sharp, keen and bright, seeing nothing but delight
on all she beheld and in all who looked
up and into them;
I always knew she saw it all,

even those times I wished she'd looked away
like when she caught us smoking in the park
and called us home to sit with her and read aloud
from the Book, about the Father who watched and waited
for the prodigal of his sons to *skrik wakker* and come on home.

But most of all, it was Grandma's soul that lit in us
an undying flame; each day the same; an endless love,
in her, a purest dove, all the way from Noah's ark
had flown and settled in her heart, and
from there, had sought to make a nest in ours…
'Love is *broos*', she'd say; God's greatest gift
made to share with infinite care with everyone;
for everyone belonged; and everyone was welcome
to find their place in the endless gracious space,
that was our beloved Grandma.

■ ■ ■

In my case, interestingly, neither of my grandmothers were anything like Grandma described above, but I have seen her in so many homes. She is the matriarchal glue that has kept families and communities together for generations. She is the home in which so many have sheltered. She is the repository of family knowledge, including the secrets she fortunately doesn't divulge. She is the keeper of the purse and, most times, of the peace too. She is the 'Ma' of the family – the mother whose presence has saved many a *laaitjie* who, like me, needed a safe harbour in the wild seas of family storms.

Upon reflection, I see many of these appealing characteristics in my own mother – a long-suffering woman who lived a life of service until she died at the age of 94. I was her last born, the one who crept into her bed at night after a scary dream. It was her long silver hair I watched being brushed as she, too briefly I always thought, sat in front of a mirror that hung on a chain from the picture rail. It was her hand one day that held my ear and marched me home after being caught smoking in the park. It was in her heart that the dove of love had made a home and sought to make a nest in mine.

I reflect on the many funerals for such Ma's I have conducted over the thirty-eight years of my ministry. Extraordinary souls departed. Each one, a pillar of stability bringing comfort, especially during dark times.

In the apartheid-filled late 1980s, together with many other clerics, I was arrested and spent a week in solitary confinement at a maximum-security prison in Cape Town. On our release, I arrived home to find the (mostly older) women of our parish tying yellow ribbons around the trees that stood in front of my small house. The women were there. All was well.

It is their strength and courage, their fortitude and resilience that is needed to fire up the revolutionary work of ushering into the world a female future. It is their capacity to love in the face of hardship and injustice that will feed us when the patriarchal resistance opposes the coming liberation. And so we celebrate them – our Ma's and Grandmas – and draw from them these essential characteristics, while at the same time, recognising their limitations.

Amongst their limitations, sadly, are that they mostly lead from behind. While they are the *de facto* leaders in many families, they often remain hidden and invisible within the structures of our communities. They're not seen in the sanctuaries of the churches. They don't sit on committees, councils or public-opinion bodies. Their influence is offered from behind the scenes, from within the kitchens and *voorkamers* of our homes. Consequently, their influence is derived from the 'moral high ground' of their eldership and the esteem in which they are held. But sadly, the rapid pace of our modern world is eating away at their high ground, weakening the authority and sometimes the relevance of their views, guidance and leadership. While honouring the lead-from-behind approach, the time for quiet diplomacy may be over.

We also need to recognise that some of the views and beliefs held by our Grandmas are themselves tinged with the stereotypical conservativism in which they grew up. The poem itself reflects several stereotypes; Grandma is found in the kitchen with flour on her *doek*. She plays traditional roles as keeper of the family recipes, the family home and the family's unity. Her maternal presence is central to the rites of passage and family celebrations, yet she seldom holds strong political views, often preferring old-fashioned chivalry, like having the door opened for her, and seeing her granddaughter in a pretty dress. She's also unlikely to engage in the complex debates about gender parity, gender assignment or sexual orientation, while wonderfully and yet ironically remaining entirely non-judgemental about her gay grandson, whom she welcomes with open arms, admitting secretly that she always knew he was 'special'. She's enigmatic and, while loving her enough to appreciate the long road she has walked, we don't have to see her as the 'complete revolutionary'.

Maybe this has been her greatest gift? That in the midst of a race-riddled, chauvinist, patriarchal world, she's been the 'safe space' in which the seeds of necessary revolution could be planted and grow so that the future becomes female. But as is always the case with revolutions, it won't arrive without sacrifice.

Mary the liberating *Theotokos*

Enter Mary, the mother of Jesus – an example of the sacrifice required. She's a woman of immense courage and insight, whose central message of freedom has been significantly watered down (of course) by the Church Fathers.

Mary, Mother of God is an archetype of liberation. She represents how revolutions are born – where they come from, so to speak – and the cost of embracing such a vision. Mary models the truth that a new future has to be born within and through us, and that it will cost us our lives.

In the Eastern Christian Church, Mary is often referred to as the *Theotokos*, the 'carrier of God'. It doesn't really matter if we are believers in *who* she was carrying within her; the point here is to realise her willingness to *give birth* to the new. It was a task she consciously agreed to, had said 'Yes' to, to which she gave her body, mind and soul. The future she dreamed of and for which she would work, was all-embracing and all-absorbing. It came from deep within, wanting to be born into this world,

to change this world. So too the future we seek. The female future needs to be formed deep within our consciousness and be born into the world. It must change everything about us, the way we live, and our being in the world. Nothing makes this clearer than the song Mary sings when, as newly pregnant, she hides in her cousin's home. Sometimes called *The Magnificat*, although I prefer the title *Ode of the Theotokos,* these are some lines summarised from the first chapter of the Gospel of Luke:

> *My soul magnifies the Lord,*
> *and my spirit rejoices in God my Saviour,*
> *for the Mighty One is about to do great things*
> *Showing strength with the arm;*
> *scattering the proud in the thoughts of their hearts.*
> *bringing down the powerful from their thrones,*
> *and lifting up the lowly; filling the hungry,*
> *and sending the rich away empty…*

It appears from the very beginning of her engagement with this cause that she understands the nature of the mission for which she's enrolling. It was going to be counter-intuitive and anti-status quo. She realises the revolutionary nature of her task. She sees it as a liberative mission: enfolding those at the edge, casting out supremacists, building a world without shame – a new reality for all humanity. But she also sees the price such a revolution could exact, and the price revolutionaries could pay – that a *'sword would one day pierce your own soul'* (Luke 2:35). Still she stands her ground, from beginning to end. She's there in the stable at the birth, and there as the cruciform shape of her first-born hangs forlorn, a crown of thorns dripping red in the darkening noon.

This poem is my small tribute to one who understood what it meant to give birth to a revolution…

Madonna

Madonna, what do you see,
who will you be,
gazing into the distance, as you do?
Is it the sword that will, in the end,
pierce your soul, as Simeon said
when you visited the temple that day?

Or is it the way
they would treat the small boy on your hip,
whose life would slip too soon away?

Or can you see him as a man
moulding a world without shame,
no-one in pain, no-one left out, where
love conquers might, and
the blind, the lame walk once again?

Or is it he, during his awakening years
mastering his heart,
learning the art, of loving without
wanting love in return?

Can you see his longing desire
for the Magdalene, his dearest
and his love for the disciple, his nearest
who lay on his shoulder at Passover
when you all gathered to eat,
but he chose instead, to wash feet?

Do you see his great tenderness, his
unending attentiveness to those at the edge
whom he pledged to enfold,
while casting out rulers
as the prophets foretold?

Or do you, perhaps, see right to the end, to
the cruciform shape of your first-born
hanging forlorn, a crown of thorns
dripping red from his head,
in the darkening noon?

Or is it of happier things?
Can you see him instead, creating a family,
a new humanity, gathered as one
light as the sun, within everyone?

If not this, what is it you see
with your mother's virgin sight?
Is it the dark path you must walk
not asking why
you should raise a son to be the one
to believe in the call

you heard at the start?

Oh Madonna, is that what you see
as you gaze pensively? A reality
few would share
with the grace to bear,
one who will suffer and die
so cruelly, so brutally, so easily, too soon?

Oh Madonna, what it must be
to see as you do…
and not close your eyes to it all.

Madonna.

One final word about Mother Mary: she's a survivor. She survives the grief of loss – the loss of her first born. As a parent who has survived the death of a child, this aspect of Mary resonates deeply with me as I'm sure it does with every parent who has experienced the anguish of losing a child. No parent should watch their child die. This form of pain can be hugely destructive and many relationships don't survive. Yet somehow, Mary, like others, found a way of transforming the pain into compassion. It can be done. All who experience the pain of oppression, or loss, or poverty, or grief, need at some point to undergo this transformation. The true revolutionaries are 'wounded healers', as spiritual writer and modern mystic Henri Nouwen called them – those whose pain has been transmuted into a compassionate passion for change.

Mary, the mercurial and enigmatic young woman from Galilee, becomes an archetypal figure for a female future. She models the awakened consciousness required for the struggle. She's a revolutionary willing to pay the price of participation. And she knows in her own heart the pain of loss and that it need not be the last word of our human experience.

Hey Madonna, what do you see, gazing into the future as you do? Do you see us free?
From the patriarchy? From chauvinism, from racism, from cultural nationalism, from homophobia, from all that diminishes and oppresses us? Hey Madonna, pray for us, please.

Mary the beloved and first *Messenger*

Mary the Mother may indeed highlight some of the attributes required by those who would be revolutionaries in the struggle for a female future. However, Mary's story remains but a story until it is experienced. We need deep personal experiences to inform and enliven our stories. And so I've chosen someone whose story, I believe, illustrates the power of personal experience. It also has an archetypal ring to it. And, yes, I'm aware that I'm a man about to tell a woman's story. But as a love story, it speaks to me too. It's the story of a woman we know today as Mary of Magdala – a close friend of Jesus of Galilee.

Much has been made of Mary of Magdala, also known as Mary Magdalene, and much has been made up about her. In the sixth century, a pope mistakenly confused her with a prostitute to whom Jesus showed immense compassion. Ever since, many have seen her as a penitent, reformed prostitute. Others say she was possessed by a demon. I'm influenced by a more progressive theology and probably, to some extent, by the compelling version of Mary in the film *Mary Magdalene* (2018), directed by Garth Davis. In this fine biblical drama, Mary is neither a prostitute, nor demon-possessed sinner. Instead she is Jesus' confidante, the witness of miracles and a voice of compassion among the other disciples, unwavering in the face of their cultural traditions and misogyny. She is the first apostle, the first messenger – one to whom Jesus chose to reveal himself after his resurrection, which is often and conveniently overlooked by the patriarchal church.

Long before I saw the film, I wrote a piece for a Good Friday Service in which I had Mary address us as follows:

> *Let me tell you who I am and, in so doing, clarify some misconceptions. I am not the prostitute some have made me out to be. That Jesus touched, healed, accepted and included prostitutes when they came to him is true. But I was not one of these, though my healing was as profound.*
>
> *I am Mary of Magdala, a small but prosperous town on the eastern shore of the Sea of Galilee. My family too were prosperous, and their wealth had bought me much of what I needed – except one thing. I will return to this later.*

I was well educated in the ways of a successful Jewish family, schooled in the basics of domestic life, concerned with the usual things of our culture, tracing my roots back several generations. My family observed the creeds and laws of Moses as did I, though I often quietly questioned why. They brought little joy or peace into my life and that of my family.

I was, outwardly, a model young Jewish woman. Inwardly, however, I suffered from an unfathomable and abiding wound – a gash in my soul that tore at the very fabric of my being – taunting me, provoking me, and robbing me of sleep, of thought and relationship. It was a darkness that overcame me from time to time – one entirely misunderstood by those around me, to whom I was but a woman, an object of the household belonging to my father and his sons. When it came, this darkness, I was lost. Roaming in the gloom, I felt not only my loneliness, but also that of generations of women who had lived before me. I feared the touch of men. I feared their ready violence, their sense of entitlement. Some said I was demon-possessed. Or they said, as did the Pharisees, that some sinful deed committed by my family had left its mark on me; that my darkness was punishment. All I knew was that one day I was fine and the next I would awake to find the dark shadow had arrived and was creeping over me – a cold shape that sucked joy, sensibility and hope from within me, leaving me fearful and uncertain. In another time, what I experienced would be called clinical depression – a psychological state compounded by the generalised trauma of the violent community in which we lived.

And then, in relationship with a Nazarene, everything changed. I cannot fully explain, other than to say I am no longer the one I was before.

Some say I'm liberated, set free. What I do know is this: that within a trusting relationship over time, I found my true sense of self, my soul, my body and my voice, and with these, my purpose. I found love and, with it, the freedom to express who I am to the world … and the confidence to enable others to do the same.

Here's another version of what I sense the remarkable Mary of Magdala felt in her heart… It's her love song.

A Love Song from Magdala

Loving One who loved me from the start as one unbroken,
whose touch when first we met lit within my heart
a spark of love, that rose above the
shadows of the night that lived in me,
freeing me to fall in love with you, as I remained

even when you died at noon before my eyes, and
in yours I saw the light go out;
but even then
I never doubted what was real to me,
all you had shared with me
those long, cold nights in which you let me keep you warm
and whispered truths about the Way of Love
I couldn't understand, until today, when

beside the tomb, you called my name, and I felt
the flame you'd lit three years before
leap anew though differently
not holding me as once you had, but rather
calling me into a deeper place of openness
in which your love, now a new and fiery gift
could enter in to burn away, burn everything away
that would hinder it from coming out

as love would want to do, that
from deep within I may share with all
the love I share with you.

A love song from Magdala

In the fight for a female future, as in every revolution, our own spirit needs to be touched by something bigger than the philosophical ideology that may have attracted us to the struggle from the start. We have seen freedom fighters brimming with ideological zeal being slowly worn down by the trauma of their endless struggle for survival. All too soon, cynicism sets in and poisons the environment. Ideology itself is insufficient for the struggle. Ideology lives in the mind, which is a good place to begin a struggle for freedom, but it's not enough. The ideology or theory of freedom needs to move into the heart and become a personal story of freedom. The heart is the meeting place of story and spirit, where passion becomes compassion, and where compassion becomes power.

The Magdalene teaches us that, without a profound personal encounter with that in which we believe – unless it has touched our hearts and changed the fabric of our experience – our vision of hope, of freedom, of a universal transformation will remain just that: a vision, a dream, an ideal, a hope.

■ ■ ■

A different future *is* possible – one in which the girl-child is central, safe and able to fulfil her potential, and so co-create an inclusive, compassionate and sustainable world. This isn't as impossible as it might seem. It starts with a radical transformation of thinking and translates into a new way of planning. My contention is this: place the girl-child at the centre of every policy. When planning health-care, put the girl-child first. Make education girl-child-centric and centred. Public safety, housing, transport, amenities, sport, tourism and travel, scholarships and bursaries, communications, the arts, entrepreneurship, financial planning – the entire fiscus needs to be based on and designed to advantage the girl-child. It is she who will lead the way. It is she who will create the world that we're waiting for.

This future mustn't be the story of a few, but rather *everyone's* story. This story isn't about gender equality. It is insufficient to call for gender parity and for the end to gender-based violence. This story isn't about women occupying equally the demeaning spaces men have created over thousands of years of patriarchal dominance. No. This is a story about 10,000 years of reimagining of the world, how we live in it and how it is managed. It is a story written on our hearts and to which every one of us can give birth. It is universal and yet deeply personal. It requires our personal and collective 'Yes', however it is said. For Rev. Dr. Jacqueline J. Lewis, a minister of the New York Middle Church, her 'yes' began with this wonderful reimagining:

> *My God is a curvy black woman with dreadlocks and dark, cocoa-brown skin. She laughs from her belly and is unashamed to cry. She can rock a whole world to sleep, singing in her contralto voice. Her sighs breathe life into humanity. Her heartbreaks cause eruptions of justice and love.*
>
> The Mendicant, Vol. 9, No.2 (2019)

■ ■ ■

I am a man born into and raised in white toxic masculinity. I have been awoken to a struggle for equality across all the divides. I seek allyship in the struggle for a female future; that I may play my part in co-creating this future. I seek to make this struggle my own and not look away.

I hope we meet on the way.

■ ■ ■

Epilogue

The day is coming when no girl-child shall tell such a vivid and sad story as this one written by D.S. Bennett, published in *The Sun* magazine in February 2002:

> *MY MOTHER always assured me that unspeakable punishments were bound to befall any child as naughty as I was.*
>
> *'If I were you,' she'd say, 'I'd be afraid to go to sleep at night, for fear God would strike me dead.' She would speak these words softly, regretfully, as though saddened by her errant daughter's fate …*
>
> *The most devastating words my mother ever spoke to me came when I asked her if she loved me. (I had just been escorted home by the police after one of my many attempts to run away, so it was bad timing on my part.) She answered, 'How could anyone ever love you?'*
>
> *It took me almost fifty years to heal the damage from all her ugly remarks.*
>
> *Recently … I related a childhood ritual of mine … From the age of five or six until I was well into my teens, whenever I had trouble sleeping, I would slip out from under my covers and steal into the kitchen for a bit of bread or cheese, which I would carry back to bed with me. There, I'd pretend my hands belonged to someone else, a comforting, reassuring being without a name — an angel, perhaps. The right hand would feed me little bites of cheese or bread as the left hand stroked my cheeks and hair. My eyes closed, I would whisper softly to myself, 'There, there. Go to sleep. You're safe now. Everything will be all right. I love you.'*

Even in the life-denying landscape of her childhood, D.S. Bennet shows that the inner source of revolution lies within. It is there, like an angel of strength waiting to arise. She also shows us that there remain among us many in need of liberation from the deeply internalised, toxic patriarchy.

Fortunately, the green shoots are forcing their way through the cracks in the sidewalk.

As this reflection ends, I'm reminded of the harrowing, but inspirational imagery used by the unmatched Ingrid Jonker (1933–1965), modern prophet as she was. In her poem, *The Child Is Not Dead,* she foresees the child become a man, walking brace and free. So too, every Girl-child… one day… not too far off…

The [Girl-]child is not dead

The girl-child is not dead, she is alive!
She has found a path,
The path is becoming a track,
The track, a roadway, and the roadway,
a highway, the highway a royal freeway
on which the girl-child is a woman
trekking across all of Africa,
a rising giant,
travelling through the whole world,
without a pass.

The girl-child is a woman!

This Curséd Violence

Turning desolation into gentle chimes of meaning

■ ■ ■

Doing a *huisbesoek* in an area rife with gang violence, I noticed dark stains on the pavement outside the parishioner's home. 'Oh,' she said when I asked, 'that's blood from the gang fight. A boy was shot last night'. Later, while in the parish church preparing for an evening meeting, this verse came to me:

They shot a boy today

They shot a boy today;
his life running out
on the road, makes
an island in the blood of war
about which our hearts,
broken a thousand times,
no longer feel pain;
our minds, trauma-cold,

forget the names of those
who carry the guns
or order the killings,
or even of the mothers whose children's
blood is on our hands
in the wars of our streets.

Expletives Deleted?

Is it ever appropriate to use expletives such as the ones that appear in some poems in this chapter?

St Peter's injunction is to exercise control over the tongue, which, if used unwisely, he says, can be a match setting alight an entire forest. The, swearing is in itself a subtle form of violence. It's like *the war on terror* – a contradiction in terms. So, on balance, swearing should probably be avoided. Is saying *'fuck the violence'* really going to shift the conversation, transform this dreadful blight on the world, or just add heat to the fire?

But I'm reminded of a potent little story told by Tony Campolo, a well-known evangelical Christian pastor and commentator. Addressing a conference of several thousand conservative Christians some years ago, he declared:

> *I have three things I'd like to say today. First, while you were sleeping last night, 30,000 kids died of starvation or diseases related to malnutrition. Second, most of you don't give a shit. Third, what's worse is that you're more upset with the fact that I said 'shit' than the fact that 30,000 kids died last night!*

Based on Campolo's story, maybe there are occasions when a swear word may be permitted? I hope you agree, for in the poems that follow, I've retained some.

I pray that we'll be more disturbed by the violence than by the expletive adjectives used to describe it.

Multiple Wounds

The scale of violence in South Africa is hard to comprehend. The structural violence of poverty and injustice, gender-based violence, child abuse, domestic violence, alcohol and drug-related violence, gang violence, road-accident violence, politically induced violence, the violence of service-delivery failure, the 'legacy violence' of our national history, the violence of corruption – and then, today, COVID-19's violent disruption of our lives and livelihoods.

Our hearts have been broken a thousand times, to the extent that we no longer feel the pain; we are numb and forget the names of those whose blood stains our streets. How can we possibly forget them? Please God, help us to remember that their lives weren't in vain: Uyinene Mrwetyana, Jesse Hess, Leighandre Jegels, Janika Mallo, Lynette Volschenk, Meghan Cremer, Anene Booysen, Noxolo Nogwaza, Valencia Farmer, Sizakele Sigasa and Salome Masooa, Janet Ntozini ... to recall only a few of the young women who have been brutally murdered.

Our hearts burn with desolation and intense rage, while pleading that a circle of protection may surround all women and children as we navigate this dark night of our collective, restless souls.

South Africa is, to borrow a diagnostic phrase from Nicaraguan psychologist Martha Cabrera, 'a multiply wounded, multiply traumatised, multiply mourning' country. Cabrera found in her own work among multiply wounded Nicaraguans that, when people's historic 'inventory of wounds' hadn't been uncovered, aired, discussed, healed and dealt with, it led to an accumulation of pain that left the entire community dysfunctional. High among the symptoms of this dysfunctionality are apathy, aggressiveness, violence, insomnia, eating disorders, intolerance, irrationality, loss of self-image, and addictive and irrational behaviour patterns – on a communal rather than just an individual scale.

Modern psychology has shown us that people who experience repeated acts of abuse, violence, shock, grief, loss – more, say, than one such event within a six-week period – are likely to develop post-traumatic stress disorder (PTSD). Moreover, those who live with ongoing PTSD may develop Continuous Traumatic Stress Disorder (CTSD) – an emotional and behavioural disorder in which a generalised numbing is the most common characteristic. South Africa today is a country enveloped by trauma, PTSD on an individual level, and CTSD on a communal level.

To address this terrible multiple wounding we need *multiple healings* – many healing interventions on multiple levels: economic, social, political, spiritual, communal and personal.

We need to be awakened from our collective numbing. Awakening to the pain is the first step of the healing path. As frightening as it is to remember the violence that courses through the veins of our broken bodies, we need to remember. We need to awaken to our hearts that are burning with desolation and rage. We need to accept our collective condition before we can begin to explore pathways for collective healing.

Having said that, however, we mustn't rush towards hope, although we need to acknowledge its importance as a source of energy for the journey. *We need to feel again,* to sit in the reality of our trauma. Denial, bargaining and anger are all part of the healing process, as is depression and desolation.

Sometimes, as we know from grief counselling, we need to process all of these emotions before some sense can be made of our trauma and loss, before acceptance and new growth can occur.

There were many flaws in the post-apartheid reconciliation process as it unfolded in the new South Africa. Maybe the largest was to use the words 'truth' and 'reconciliation' in such close proximity – as if the discovery of truth automatically leads to reconciliation. Between these two powerful concepts are several other important steps, such as acknowledging, lamentation (weeping), justice, restoring, restitution, healing, and nurturing. In my view, reconciliation has little chance of taking root without these other intermediate phases being addressed.

The poems that follow are of remembrance, of anger, and of desolation. They reflect the wide range of grief, loss and trauma – all personal, yet all generic – and remind us of our long, hard path to healing.

To frame these poems, and because I believe that the hope of healing exists in all of us, I start with a poem of outrage and hope, using the voices of women I have heard in my head and my heart...

This Cursed Violence

This Curséd Violence

A young widow:
Fuck this curséd violence
that sent my lover to his grave;
Fuck these wars fought by men
Fuck their drums of rage
Fuck their guns, bullets, their gangs
that fuel my endless pain.

A women's group:
Fuck this curséd violence
turning all we hold to dust
Fuck the laws that don't protect us
from the men who bind and rape us
Fuck these days of fear and shame,
that feed our endless pain.

A woman gang member:
Fuck this curséd violence
that's crept deep within me
Fuck it's unforgiving grudges
that makes me do to others
what they've done to me,
with their endless pain.

A girl-child:
Wait, my sisters, listen my mothers…
Hear my words, though not mine, but ours;
Amidst the lies, our dark-rimmed eyes disguise
what we know to be true, that;
no more can their savage acts enrol
us in a silence as evil as their violence.

No more shall this be the story of our lives!
No more shall we fold our hands while another cries!
No more shall we be the fill their belly desires!
No more shall we be owned by another,
be abused by a father or a brother!
For today, we take our places
with our bruised and bloodied faces,
and cry as one, for every *man*.
Yes, every solitary *man*,
to hear our universal call…

We will end this curséd violence!
We will end its endless pain!

Our time has come,
Our will will be done,
On earth as in our hearts,

For today, our liberation starts;
We can hear our freedom beckoning
to end this curséd violence;

Today begins the reckoning
of our combined connivance!

Today, tomorrow, and the next
we shall not rest,
until our songs of freedom become
the universal anthem
and this curséd violence
ends for all!

Pledged to Serve and Protect?

Among the deaths that outraged me is that of Nateniël Julies, a young man born with Down's syndrome.

He was shot one evening by the police as he struggled to make his way home from a nearby park. At the time of writing the trial of his alleged murderers is ongoing. His grief-stricken family waits for justice, for their pain to end, and their experience of the curséd violence to heal.

Who shot Nateniël?

Hey you, you who shot the kid,
Do you know what you did?
Could you not see
the boy, unlike the rest,
doing his best, to get away,
was different?

What was so unclear, that
you failed to see him standing there, near
the gate he had to open,
his fingers struggling
to undo the bolt
that locked him
in your sight, the night
you shot and killed him?

Could you not tell
he was confused
by your orders in the dark,
at the park
in which his friends,
unlike you, knew him well

when you say you shouted 'Stop!'
and then shot at him?

You say you couldn't see that
he was born
with Down syndrome?
Well, what else don't you see
in those on your beat, those
you've pledged to
serve and protect?

But instead you, you show up
blue lights flashing, guns a-blazing,
shooting to kill
a boy with Down syndrome
struggling to go home
up the hill...

What's so agitating, is
you don't seem to know
what you've done
or give a fuck?

The Sacrificial Love of a Hero

Most violent deaths are incomprehensible, including that of a true hero of humankind: Janet Ntozini. Janet, a beautiful teenager from Vrygrond, Cape Town, was stabbed to death while trying to protect a physically disabled [differently abled] boy in her neighbourhood from being attacked by an older man. Speaking to a journalist, Janet's grandmother, Novusile Ntozini, is reported to have said: 'God comforts me with the knowledge that my child died helping a disabled teenager. Thinking about that makes me strong and gives me peace.' She described Janet as a kind and caring person who did not have an easy upbringing. Her nature was such that she couldn't stand watching bad things happen to other people; she was always the first to help other people: 'She died because of helping a person, she always believed in protecting people.'

Janet's act of selflessness resonates so profoundly with the words of Jesus of Nazareth: 'There is no greater love than to lay down one's life for one's friends.' While this may be true, it doesn't take away the pain and loss – the senseless loss.

In Janet's actions we see the meaning of love, the courage of love, the nature of love, and the cost of love. In Janet's death, we see the meaningless of violence, the suddenness of death, the fragility of life, and how thin the thread is that holds us to this reality we call ours. Small wonder we run away or at least turn away from the drama of trauma in our midst.

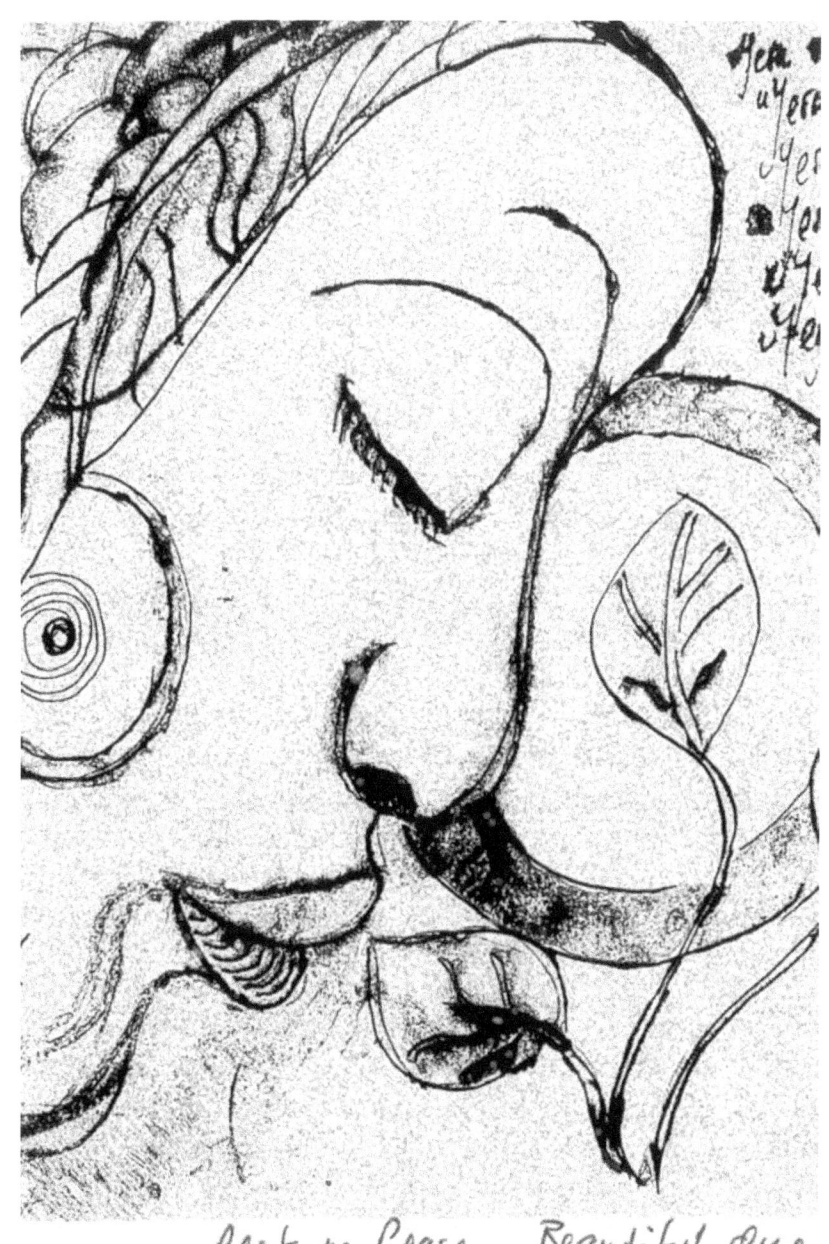
Rest in Peace, Beautiful One

Rest In Peace, Beautiful One

Rest in peace, Janet Ntozini, beautiful one,
Young Champion of Humankind,
and pray for us.
For unlike you, we're so afraid to act, to die
for what is right; and instead
become bystanders, numbed participants
in this curséd violence.

■ ■ ■

Parcels of Love

The death of a child – even from natural causes – frequently results in the break-up of marriages. No one escapes the scar. It is an excruciatingly painful wound. The murder of a child is almost unbearable and must be the single most traumatic life-event a parent could ever have to endure.

A murder that shook South Africa was that of Uyinene Mrwetyana, a University of Cape Town student. She went one day to collect a parcel from the local post office. There, alone, a postal worker brutally and savagely murdered her.

'Uyi-uyi', as she was known to her loved ones, was a young woman with enormous promise, huge potential, and a love of life and all around her. Her bubbly personality was said to be infectious. Like many young women today, she was outspoken on a range of social ills affecting the lives of so many of her compatriots in the struggle to build a safe and equitable world. She had spoken out loudly against patriarchal oppression and gender-based violence.

At the time of Uyinene's death, our younger daughter Zoë, was studying at the university currently known as Rhodes University in Makhanda in the Eastern Cape; in which Uyinene's mother holds a senior position. It so happened that, at that time, I had recently sent Zoë a parcel filled with delicacies and surprises – something I had been promising to do for some time. And so it was that both Uyinene and Zoë would collect parcels: Uyinene collecting hers in Zoë's home town, and Zoë in Uyinene's home town.

I don't know the details of the parcel Uyinene went to collect, or its contents, but the extraordinary similarities were overwhelming.

The Parcel

The parcel she went to collect
the one that took her life
and broke my heart

The one I packed with
joy-filled things
to show her how much I miss her
and how well I know
the things she loves
just as was she

The one I loved
the moment she was

wrapped in sacred secret love
within my womb
as only a mother understands
and sends into the world

Only to be snatched
one cold stark day,
caught and robbed
torn open, broken, battered,
emptied, caste aside
by a man from whom
she went to fetch
the parcel of my love –
who stole the parcel of my love.

■ ■ ■

Reflecting on Uyinene's death, I tried to place myself in the Mrwetyanas' tragic and desperate situation – trying to find words to describe firstly the pain of a mother losing her beloved daughter, and secondly my belief (I so want to believe this) that at the end, Uyinene never doubted the love with which she had been loved all her short lif

A Daughter's Response

Mama, I'm sorry
to break your heart;
to die the way I did,
so tragically,
before my time

Though the way
you looked at me
as we kissed goodbye, last time,
I wondered if you feared
the worst for me?
A mother's intuition?

I often wondered
how we'd ever say goodbye?
For no-one had love
so deep, so round,
so endless
as was your love for me

So take heart my dearest Ma
standing so silent at my grave,
though torn and broken
as I was
of your sweet love
parcelled deep
within my heart.

Be assured,
it was there,

your deep, round special love was there
and it gave me breath throughout,
throughout it all.

And when at last,
through the darkness
the sweet light came,
none of it was lost;
none of your sweet love was lost.

The Sweet Children We Fail

For some time after joining the Diocese of Saldanha Bay, I had pastoral responsibilities in an area of Elsie's River on the Cape Flats that included Eureka and Connaught Estates. The two *'estates'* are especially tough areas, where poverty is endemic, as is violence. The residents speak fondly of their 'township', living alongside the hardship with exceptional resilience. I learnt a lot about traumatic disorders while ministering there, as well as remarkably courageous and beautiful people. Sadly, violent death was never far away.

For Tazne van Wyk, a little eight-year-old girl from Connaught Estate, death came at the hands of a neighbour who had been released from prison after serving just half of his 10-year sentence for culpable homicide and kidnapping. It was this parolee who somehow lured Tazne to a violent and harrowing death. The perpetrator was eventually arrested and is back behind bars, but due to pressure on the courts, the trial continues to be postponed. South Africa's dysfunctional justice system not only paroled a violent man too soon, but also, when he was arrested for yet another heinous crime, has delayed prosecution for over two years. For the Van Wyk family, their trauma goes on and on while they wait for some form of closure.

The thought of a beautiful little girl walking down the road to buy sweets from the local *babbie-shop* and not returning for days, only to be found murdered and badly mutilated in a storm-water drain some 120 kilometres away, is too dreadful for words.

When I heard the news, not only did my heart break for little Tazne's parents and family, but I felt an overwhelming sense of collective grief and failure: not only had the justice system failed her, but *we, together, everyone* had failed her.

While Tazne's alleged murderer awaits trial, culpability for her death, in some measure, has to lie at our collective feet. The dark violence that lives in her murderer isn't his alone.

It has its roots in our neglect, in our refusal to swim against the tides of the 'I-come-first' ego-centric world we have constructed. This isn't a *bleeding-heart appeal* for clemency. Let justice take its course! But what sort of world is it that created this murdering monster?

And when he's found guilty and imprisoned for life, what sort of world will it be then? Will justice have been served? Sweet Tazne's death may have been avenged but will her sweet life have been restored? Has retribution ever delivered justice?

And has our retributive justice system delivered less child murders today than yesterday? Is it possible, maybe to ask what restoration could look like in this context?

For Tazne, Sweet Child of Ours

Sweet child of ours
whom we've failed and lost;
About whose final hours
we fear to ask...
What darkness did you endure?

Did the pain burn your soul?
Were you cold and alone?

Did you hear the cries from home?
Was the crossing hard to do?
Could you see
a path to tread, to the light
from the dread
of your imprisonment?

How did we let you go,
just slip away into the night
as we did before, when
Stacha Arendse, Courtney Pieters,
Shaynice Talla, Vuyokazi Mgolodela
disappeared just like you?

And as we add your beloved name:
Tazne van Wyk, aged eight, Connaught Estate
to the list of those who have died
and those our prayers couldn't save;
Will we stop and face the truth,
the open wound, you've laid bare?

That the darkness within
the one who took your life
has its roots in our neglect,
in our refusal to swim upstream,
against the tides
of I-Come-First!

And will we see that
we're the ones we're waiting for,
now's the time we're longing for;
that it's up to us
to shape this world

for girls aged eight to walk alone
to the shop
not far from home
without a care and
without fear?

Oh sweet child of ours,
pray for us
for we have failed and are lost…

Pictures of the Heart

Parish priests grow accustomed, sadly, to receiving sad news over the phone. Like rural doctors or social workers, priests are often called to make haste to a home or hospital where someone is in need, or a family is gathered in shocked silence trying to comprehend the sudden death of a loved one.

After such a phone call, a few years ago, I sat in the home of dear parishioner in Parow, Cape Town, listening as the sad events of the night were revealed.

A dear son, the younger of two, had heard news that a friend was being accosted nearby. Rushing to his friend's defence, he himself was confronted and fatally wounded, dying at the scene.

In the sitting room with us as we shared the grim details, was Cayden, the deceased's son, a boy of twelve. Bravely he listened to the story and, over the following days, to the plans we made for his father's funeral.

This mindless death of a vibrant young man who had come to terms with so many of his own demons reminded me of the fragility of life and the suddenness with which death disrupts our lives. It is so abrupt sometimes. On the death of a loved one, the separation feels so final. Many want to have one last encounter, exchange one last squeeze of the hand, kiss a still-warm cheek, say some final words of farewell or thanks. When we don't have these opportunities, the finality of death is even harder to accept.

On the day of the funeral, shocked community members arrived in numbers to mourn the passing of their brave friend. The church was full. I watched as the family took their places in the front pew. Sitting just to the right of the coffin was the young, equally brave Cayden. I recall thinking just how poised he looked – stoical in his grief – alongside his bereft mother, grandmother and aunt.

A large framed photo of his the deceased had been placed on the coffin – a somewhat recent custom I have encouraged over the years. Funerals are so important in the processing of grieving. The old notion that a funeral should be a solemn, unemotional opportunity is thankfully making way for funerals that are significant moments of celebration and grief – a time for sharing stories and memories of the loved one, for the full range of emotions, and for poignantly taking leave of the body of our loved one while commending their spirit into the hands of the Source of Love.

Alongside the opportunities for sharing stories at funerals, in the Anglican tradition, some beautiful prayers are prayed towards the end of the service, during which, sometimes, the coffin is blessed with water. Water is the archetypal symbol of life – in which we lived *in utero,* with which we are washed at birth, and in which we are baptised – making it an important symbol to have present at the end. This is one of the beautiful prayers that are said:

> *May the angels lead you into paradise;*
> *May the martyrs come to welcome you and take you to the new and eternal Jerusalem.*
> *May the choir of angels welcome you;*
> *Where Lazerus is poor no longer,*
> *May you have eternal rest. Amen.*

At Cayden's father's funeral, after saying this particular prayer, I invited the pallbearers to come forward to usher the coffin from the church. The undertaker came forward to assist in this final act, and taking the picture from the coffin, he noticed Cayden standing in the front pew. Reaching over, he carefully placed the framed photograph into Cayden's hands.

The weight of the moment was too much. The floodgates of emotion that Cayden had so bravely held at bay throughout the ceremony broke and, holding the photograph to his heart, he wept.

The image of this young son of the son we were burying, weeping, is forever etched in my memory.

This poem is for you, Cayden…

At His Father's Funeral

So silent he sat at his father's funeral
I wonder what he heard
of our prayers and psalms,
his fists pushing against the tears
as we sang our songs
and shared our sad fears
of his father whose sudden
death last Friday night, shocked us all.

I watched him, there, in the pew
alone beside his mother
whose days with his father had been too few.
So much his heart had to enfold,
it was bound to break, and did

as the photo of his father
like a baton that it was
placed upon the coffin lid
was passed to him to hold.

And, as he took the picture frame
and held it to his chest
he broke and wept
the lonely tears of grief
we all were holding back.

In that moment of despair,
I saw in him a truth we each must hear;
That at the end,
all we can hold of those we love
are the pictures we have framed
through the years, of them
in our hearts.

※ ※ ※

This poem seeks primarily, to capture something of the immense grief that washed though a son at his dad's funeral. It was a funeral of immense sadness for us all. Not only was this the funeral of a young man who remarkably had managed to turn his somewhat prodigal life around and was making good, but it was also the funeral of a brave friend who had laid down his life for another. Outside the church, unable to come inside, were two tough-looking but broken-hearted former friends who felt the great injustice and sadness of it all.

In the end, I hope the poem reminds us of the delicate thread that holds us and those we love to our current reality – a thread that so easily and instantly in some cases, is broken.

We have only the moments of each day to affirm those we love. When they are gone, all we will have, if we are lucky, are the pictures we have framed of them in our hearts.

Exhausted Hearts and Our TV Screens

As the world, gripped by the COVID-19 pandemic, watches millions of people dying, our eyes are diverted from the grim death caused by famine, pollution, and the insidious mindless violence of war.

One of the tragic by-products of our constant exposure to trauma is the generalised exhaustion – collective numbing – that saps our empathy and energy. Frontline medical workers have to deal with the constant bombardment of sick and dying patients. In the end, it is hard to stay emotionally present to such incessant suffering.

While the presence of this kind of exhaustion has been exacerbated by the pandemic, we have experienced it before. Ever since Bob Geldof opened our eyes to starving children in the brutal Ethiopian famine in 1985, we have been exposed to pictures of dying people in wars, in refugee camps, in makeshift and poorly equipped hospitals, and the like. From natural events like earthquakes and tsunamis, to scenes of frightened refugees carrying their meagre possessions into exile, we have been barraged by imagery of suffering. Sometimes we may be moved to donate money, to sign a petition, to join a street protest.

In some cases, the media coverage has rightly and powerfully encouraged us to engage in society-changing acts of revolution, as in the 'must-fall' and 'spring' movements. We should be grateful for the role the Fourth Estate plays in documenting the horrors and injustices that occur daily around the world, and for promoting the core values of a just, inclusive society. Courageous, fact-driven journalism that searches for and broadcasts the truth is the oxygen of the human rights movement.

I have, for years, felt desperate about the war in Syria. It is a despicable war – made worse by its proxy nature – by superpowers who use and abuse Syrian politics for their own eco-political agendas. Making it worse is the wanton destruction of this ancient land and its historic legacy.

This land and culture traces its roots back to the tenth century BCE. Archaeological evidence, such as the skeleton of a Neanderthal two-year-old child who lived in the Middle Palaeolithic era (c. 200,000 to 40,000 years ago), illustrates the significance of this part of the world.

Our current disregard for the pre-history of our world belies much of our present abuse of our planet and each other. We have forgotten the precious nature of the orb on which we live, with its rich evolving mysteries, myths and history – all of which are essential pointers for us as we seek to craft our future. Without knowledge of our common past, our efforts to build a common future are significantly diminished. We know this to be true!

And so, in the present Syrian war, we are witnessing the destruction of history, of civilisation, of cities and peoples, of thousands upon thousands of human stories, and doing very little about it. We seem exhausted by it all; numbed to the suffering. An example of this, it seems to me, was the discovery of another child from that region. Alan Kurdi was a three-year old boy of Kurdish background, fleeing with his family on a questionably seaworthy boat. Alan was born in Kobane, Syria – the site of the Kobani Massacre – itself a gruesome killing field. Having fled that horror, little Alan drowned off the Turkish coast.

The picture of his lifeless body lying face-down on the beach was flashed across the world and joins other photographic icons of suffering: Kevin Carter's 'The Struggling Boy' (a collapsed Sudanese child watched by a hooded vulture), Nick Ut's 'The Terror of War' (also known as 'Napalm Girl', showing children fleeing a napalm bombing during the Vietnam War), and Sam Nzima's historic Soweto uprising photograph of Zolile Hector Pieterson being carried home on 16 June 1976.

I sat with Nilüfer Demir's picture of little Alan for a long time. There he lay being watched over by two Turkish policemen, helpless, like me, like everyone, like his father: shocked, numb, exhausted by the ongoing suffering of the people of the greater Syrian region and the complexity of it all. The fleeing continues, as does the hostile reception on their arrival in southern Europe.

I wanted to commemorate this tragedy – to somehow mark both Alan's horrific death and the endless Syrian war. In addition, I sought to say something about our exhausted inability to do something about it...

Alan Kurdi's 'Sister'

Clinging arms and cries
from a darkened watery world, she's plucked –
God's arm, just long enough, this time
to reach her, their girl,
her Syrian boat upturned
as is her warring, falling world
we see on our TV screens.

Fleeting prayers and thoughts,
float across my mind
not long enough
to make the world take note of them,
these refugees,
hoping to live another day,
one more than Alan, their boy,
washed ashore,
his journey's end a
public scene
beamed on our TV screens
some days before,
as if we care.

Alan Kurdi's Sister

The Violence of Poverty

In 2018, a group of wonderfully energetic people walked the 130 kilometres from Saldanha Bay to Elands Bay. It took us six days, hiking mostly on the beach, and either sleeping rough or staying with families from the local communities (and for two nights in rather luxurious lodges!). We called it 'The Weskus Camino' and one day it could become a regular feature. For those who know it, the Weskus is breathtakingly awe-inspiring and frighteningly hostile. It is perfect terrain for a spiritual experience, with its long lonely beaches, sun-baked salt pans, wind-swept sand dunes, and tussled grasses. I've been visiting the Weskus for over forty years, especially the old fishing village of Stofbergsfontein (also known incorrectly as Churchhaven) on the shores of the Langebaan Lagoon, within the West Coast National Park. I once wrote a poem addressing the mysterious, ever-changing lagoon, the first verse of which went like this:

> *Will I ever find the words to tell you*
> *how you've shaped my life each day;*
> *or of the colours you assume;*
> *each morning's view different, unlike before;*
> *azure sparkling shafts, like stolen silver arrows*
> *reflecting love's delight; then sudden black*
> *unyielding, deadly in embrace;*
> *then loamy grey, as one undressed in innocence;*
> *then flimsy teardrops falling from angels on their slow swoop home;*
> *then breathless kisses of foam cupping lilting breasts, all smiles;*
> *your finely fashioned fingers*
> *lapping longingly on supine shores?*

the violence of poverty

It is easy to romanticise the Weskus. It is beautiful, but it is also and always has been a site of struggle, of fishermen losing their lives in the sudden storms that hurl five-metre waves against the rocky shores, of fish-factory workers earning a pittance for the catches they spend hours processing, of the farmworkers paid in *dop,* of the alcohol abuse and associated violence, of miners living in tin shacks as the wealth of the diamonds and minerals they mine is ferreted away by mine bosses with their overseas' company listings and diamond encrusted rings. Indeed, the Weskus can be a very hard place, especially for an unemployed, poverty-stricken, yet enormously courageous widower trying to raise his children. His name is Albertus Swartz and we found him on the sand dunes outside a Weskus *dorpie*. Albertus represents millions of South Africans who are confronted daily by the violence of poverty. Systemic poverty in a land of plenty is a crime against humanity, and everyone who has access to daily sufficiency is on trial for this crime.

Poverty is an issue where we need to 'think global and act local'. From a global perspective, we need global solutions, such as implementing and attaining the United Nations Sustainable Development Goals for 2030, the first of which is 'No Poverty'.

We need international, interconnected solutions to these interconnected and interwoven social pathologies. We need counties to comply with the charters and agreements and strategies. We need political will and revolutionary citizen agitation. We also need loads more thinking, debate and decision-making about new economic models for a sustainable world. The crass exploitation, manufacturing and consumption-based model, like the patriarchy, has brought enormous wealth to a few, but to the majority it has delivered enormous disparity and hardship.

New socio-economic models *are* being developed and *are* feasible. My own preference is for the model developed and promoted by the award-winning economist Kate Raworth, which is rather spiritedly called 'Doughnut economics'. She is calling for a new visual map to represent the future – one that moves away from linear thinking, from the upward moving 'line of progress' ingrained in us all, to a 'regenerative and distributive' model designed to engage everyone. And it's shaped like a doughnut! On her website (www.kateraworth.com), she explains:

> *Humanity's 21st century challenge is to meet the needs of all within the means of the planet. In other words, to ensure that no one falls short on life's essentials (from food and housing to*

healthcare and political voice), while ensuring that collectively we do not overshoot our pressure on Earth's life-supporting systems, on which we fundamentally depend – such as a stable climate, fertile soils, and a protective ozone layer. The Doughnut of social and planetary boundaries is a playfully serious approach to framing that challenge, and it acts as a compass for human progress this century.

Locally, you and I need to act against waste, against greed, against hoarding, against indiscriminate consumerism. Let's become pro-sharing, pro-community action, proactive, concerned and introspective individuals, regularly auditing our arrogant consumption habits.

Every salaried person should be giving generously to, among other things, community-based and credible poverty eradication programmes. Become a vegetarian (which is both a local action that may save your life, and a global action that will reduce our collective dependence on unsustainable and cruel animal faming). Stop smoking and spend the money on a vegetable garden. Quit buying fast foods and fizzy drinks, and engage in random acts of kindness like buying two or more *Big Issues* a month. Pick up litter. Reduce, reuse, recycle. Support a circular economy by buying local and sharing things you don't need or use. Support charity shops and community farming projects. Limit your carbon footprint by walking more. Educate your children about the importance of eradicating poverty from the world. And *then*, if you're doing *all* of this... *then* you can moan about corrupt governments that aren't doing enough. But not before!

Poverty is violent. It kills, stunts, robs, assaults, invades, rapes, abuses children, mothers, anyone, everyone who gets in its way. It denies its victims their most fundamental human right: to fulfil their God-given potential and be able to give all of their gifts to the world!

After meeting and spending time talking with Albertus Swartz, his face etched on my mind, the feel of his rough-chapped hands on mine, his lonely story going around in my heart, I wrote this poem:

Ode to Albertus

Albertus Swartz, on the Weskus
a soldier of poverty, working
the dunes, searching for copper
he'll trade to take home, as
food for his children, living alone
since his wife died that past year.

We found him, surprised him,
a man in the mist as it rolled from
the sea, onto the dunes,
where he rakes the scorched sand
each day, the same
since the mines closed and left.

We stopped and we watched
our bodies warm in our coats
damp from the air, his hands
calloused and cold, from digging
the scraps he'll be dealing
with traders who pawn what he finds.

We greeted and spoke, this
father, finder, soldier
of poverty, and we, visitors
of plenty, hearing his words, had
nothing to say, wanting to run away
from one of many long left behind.

Ode to Albertus

> We parted then, each going our way
> caught in the moment of
> that autumn grey
> morning encounter, enveloped in
> anger, desperation and pain, silenced
> by the presence of God we saw in this man
> calling us to act

■ ■ ■

As I read the poem and recall this encounter, I accept the patronising sentiment expressed in the last verse: *that the presence of God we saw in this man is calling us to act.*

Then we leave with our anger, desperation and pain silenced, and climb back into the comfort of our 'developed-world' existence. I'm so compromised by the security of my privilege; I feel so powerless in the face of this juggernaut. And yet in young people, we can see a new realism, a new willingness to turn their backs on cold, rabid capitalism and the destruction of our planet. Indeed, we can see the shoots of new activism and new behaviours across the issues we are facing.

American poet, Alison Luterman, once wrote a powerful poem titled 'The New Breed' about a young woman…

> *… screaming into a microphone,*
> *Her head is shaved and she is beautiful*
> *and seventeen …*

She's outraged at the murder of her friends in a school shooting and

> *… in the fullness of her young fire,*
> *calling bullshit on politicians who take money from the gun-makers.*

And you can see the gray faces of those
who have always held power
contort, utterly baffled to face this new breed of young woman, …
we say to each other,
Well, it looks like the baton
may be passing …

The baton *is* passing and I'm a believer in those coming after me, who are growing in number and consciousness, seeking a new, fair, just, inclusive and sustainable world.

And at a national level, I'm an enthusiastic disciple of the basic income grant, believing in its immediate implementation for all South Africans between the ages of 18 and 59, to be paid for through public taxation. No question!

Silent Violence

There is one last aspect of violence on which I would like to reflect – not that we have come near to exhausting its multiple forms and shapes. While corruption and the callous destruction of our planet (environmental degradation) are among the many voracious, vicious and prevalent forms of violence that should be called out and confronted, there is a silent violence that touches many, regardless of their race, station, gender and geography.

It is illness – terminal illness. It has many savage faces, all of which disfigure, scar and mortally wound those it visits.

My sister, Barbara, the younger of two sisters and the third-born of my siblings, died from cancer. She received the diagnosis four months before she died; it was in her lungs – stage 4, the most advanced.

The silent, violent killer had been stalking her for a considerable time before making its presence felt.

Palliative care was the only real option.

My wife, Jacqui, and I were travelling in India when she shared the news with us. As is my coping pattern in these circumstances, I went into a form of denial and looked desperately for some silver lining among the storm clouds.

That morning I wrote a poem, placing in her mouth the words I hoped would be hers – indeed the words I wanted to hear given the grim reality she was facing.

For our sister, Barbs

I shall surely die
as they know too,
whose voices share
concern for me
since we received the news.

But I shall die a noble death
although it be too soon.
Mine, a joyful end
although with hospice veil.
I shall laugh
although my lips don't move
and I shall sing
although no sound rings out.

Light shall shine through this,
although my body fails;
although the air be thin to draw;
although my hope wears out
although it looks like night.

Through all of this,
with thoughts and prayers,
and the arms of those who will
hold and help me,
I shall get through this.

Epilogue

Violence can be defined in three ways: as a form of behaviour involving physical force intended to hurt, damage or kill someone or something; as the strength of emotion (violent feelings like hate and rage); and as a destructive natural force (a volcano, a tsunami, or even a pandemic). Except for a few violent acts of nature, we have a measure of control over the rest. We can control our behaviour. We can control our emotions. We increasingly see that our actions can control acts of nature – like climate change, for example. As Nelson Mandela said in his *Long Walk to Freedom*: 'No one is born hating ... People must learn to hate, and if they can learn to hate, they can be taught to love, for love comes more naturally to the human heart than its opposite.'

Violence isn't in our design. Our original face, a vivid Zen term for our original nature, is one of beauty, of goodness, of intrinsic kindness. We've forgotten this. We've forgotten what we look like. Our task is to awaken from this forgetfulness and, in recovery, to discover who we are and build a world in which violence becomes but a shameful part of our evolving human story – something in the annals of history that our children will read about with amazement.

It is a sacred awakening to which we are all being called. On behalf of all whose personal stories illustrate the collective story of our societies; on behalf of all who feel they have become the detritus of war, displaced and disposable; on behalf of all who are excluded, violated, humiliated, Patricia Schonstein Pinnock in her magnificent book *Skyline* hears them saying:

> *Turn our desolation into something memorable. That it may not have been in vain to lose what little we owned. Make for our lost children a chime of gentle sound that they might follow it and escape, one day, from the plateau of war.*

That we may be that chime of gentle sound that enables all to escape the plateau of violence,

Lord, in your mercy,
Hear our prayer.

Did God Give Me This?

Finding a home in the land of otherness

■ ■ ■

A THAI TEMPLE once housed the largest clay Buddha statue in the land. Though not the most beautiful statue – for there were many – it had been lovingly cared for down the generations by diligent and faithful monks from the nearby monastery. Violent storms, changes of government and even wars, the clay Buddha had endured. Then one day, the local monks noticed a large crack in the giant statue. Concerned, they hurriedly informed their Abbot, who in turn sent a team to see what could be done to repair their beloved clay statue. With his lantern in hand, the most qualified of monks peered into the crack and, to his surprise, was dazzled by a flash of gold. After cautiously chipping away the clay, he exposed, beneath the clay covering, the largest and most beautiful golden Buddha in all of Thailand. Upon further historical research they learned that, during a particularly severe time of conflict, a previous generation of monks had covered their golden statue with clay in order to make it appear dowdy, uninteresting and undesirable – an object no marauding army would want to steal, own or damage.

I first heard this story from Jack Kornfield, a popular Buddhist psychologist and teacher. He rightly uses it to explain a profound truth the story illustrates. Each of us is a golden Buddha – intrinsically and inherently pure gold, beautiful, and of inestimable worth. This is our essential human condition – our 'original face' as it is described in Zen. This is who we are as we are 'being formed in the sacred places of the earth' as the Jewish poets described it.

We are originally blessed, as Christian priest and writer Matthew Fox likes to say. Richard Rohr, another popular Christian teacher, beautifully describes this inner dimension of our humanity, this inner-me, as an 'immortal diamond'. Discovering and uncovering this diamond, and presenting it to the world, is our most profound life task.

Removing the Clay

Through our life experiences, we learn to apply the clay, covering our true nature or 'true-self' as mystic Thomas Merton calls it. What we present to the world is not who we truly are – it is the clay covering we have so diligently applied. This clay version of our self, some call the false-self, the little-self, or the socialised-self. I prefer to describe it as the ego-self.

What we have learned is that the ego-self is covered not merely with the clay of our own personal experiences, but by a whole range of inherited or collective experiences into which we are born. In the Old Testament, we read that the sins of the forefathers are visited upon the children's children to the third and fourth generation. Often referred to as the generational curse, it's not so much a curse as, sadly, a statement of fact. Carl Jung, a co-founding father of modern psychology used the term 'collective unconscious' to refer to the psychological material we inherit from our parents and from the society into which we are born. Geneticists today are more and more certain that the genes, which determine the colour of our eyes and myriad other physical characteristics, also carry a host of psychological data that will provide each of us with a unique temperament predisposition. This temperament interacts with the forces of socialisation to determine our preferences and behaviours.

Awakening to Our Original Face

Each of us has an original face, a golden Buddha deep within. It is unique, inviolable and whole. Merton called this 'a hidden wholeness deep within'. James Finley, another modern mystic, called it the 'innermost centre of our self'. In traditional theology the Latin phrase *Imago Dei* – the Image of God –is used to describe this essential gift that lives within us. Today we call it the true-self – that inner, inalienable part of us blessed by an original blessing from the Source of Life and Love who some call God. It is a gift and it is within every sentient being. For we who are *homo sapiens*, it is the core of our humanity – an essence beyond abstraction and yet so ethereal it is beyond all constriction or destruction. Nothing – not violence, not hunger or thirst, not alienation or illusion, not any form of abuse, visited by self or another, not even death – can destroy this essential original face.

This wondrous gift deep within comes packaged in human form – born as an infant, a bundle of physical and emotional needs, longings and requirements. By definition, the infant's modus operandi is to attract and demand attention to meet its primary needs. It clings and grasps and latches, drinks and grabs – seeking and needing to be held, to be attached to its caregiver. This attachment is vital, and the degree to which the infant feels positively attached, sufficiently attached, will be the degree to which, one day, it will release its clasping need to belong to another and become a happy, adjusted individual.

The driving force in the infant's early years is what is often described as the ego-self. This self is designed to ensure the infant has access to what it needs to survive and thrive. The ego-self is pretty much focused on survival, getting what it needs, and remaining at the centre of what it perceives as the universe. Another helpful way of describing the nature of the ego-self is to see it as wrapped in dense consciousness. It is solid, tight, clenched. It has to be; that's its role and purpose. Stay focused on staying alive. It is the 'me-first' world of the toddler and even the teenager, and sadly of many egocentric adults who remain in the realm of ego-self.

It is through this ego-self that we begin to experience the world – a world filled with 'ten thousand joys and ten thousand sorrows' as the Buddha so aptly suggested. With each joy the ego-self relaxes and releases its clenched-fist control, and with each sorrow the ego-self builds defences and finds ways of protecting itself. Sorrows that are too deep, too large, break through the defensive barriers, causing inner wounds and the ego-self to contract. And so the clay is applied.

Within all of this – deeply buried in the midst of the unawakened dense-consciousness, surrounded by the defences of wounding experiences – lies our original face, inner wholeness, the immortal diamond, the true-self, waiting to be discovered, uncovered, recovered. It may be that we once had knowledge of this true-self – perhaps a fleeting encounter in our mother's womb, or in some pre-existent life experience – but by the time we're born, we've forgotten it, lost touch with it, are asleep to it. Our task is to *awaken*, to remember, to search and to discover our true-self, and disentangle it from the ego-self's world of grasping and defending. As we give ourselves to this process, we are increasingly enveloped in a light-consciousness – a world of greater fluidity, openness, joyful exploration, meaning and purpose. To discover our original face and wear it proudly in the world is to experience our humanity in its fullness. Many social forces conspire to inhibit this awakening and discovery. Poverty, oppression, discrimination, inequity, illness and violence impact enormously on our ability to engage on our hero's journey of finding our original face. Painful experiences are internalised and harden the shell of our dense consciousness, setting back our discovery.

To maintain control and protect positions of privilege, various social systems like the patriarchy, colonialism, apartheid and religious doctrines developed ways of preventing the journey of awakening from taking place. One of these ways was the creation of labels and constructs that would be applied to certain peoples in order to segregate and subjugate them. Race theory, gender and sexuality labelling are examples. Of course, it is true that scientific reductionism used labels and constructs in helpful ways. To dissect and identify, to inspect and discover, were essential parts of modernism and post-modern rationalism, which brought breakthroughs in health, engineering, communications, and the like. But everything has its shadow. The application of labels has been used to subjugate, wound, kill or destroy much of creation, especially humans.

Sometimes we have to reinvent the labels and give them new and powerful meanings in order to transform them from a means of oppression into vehicles for liberation. This is no truer than in the complex world of human sexuality. The labels 'homosexual' (or today, 'lesbian' and 'gay') – which are still used widely as a reason to criminalise, oppress and reject people – have been transformed into rallying cries and labels of freedom by those who find this to be the authentic expression of their humanity.

A Bystanders' Commission

As an Anglican priest, it has been deeply distressing for many years to witness the church's inability to come to terms with an essential truth: that within every person there is an original face or true-self waiting to emerge and be worn with pride and beauty in the world. As part of the process, every label that inhibits this joyful liberation needs either to be discarded or transformed into a means of freedom. As a Christian, I am in no doubt that this is what St Paul's words meant when he wrote to the people of Galatia (3:28): 'There is neither Jew not Greek [Gentile], slave nor free, male nor female, for you all are one in Christ Jesus'. Though this is but one verse, it represents a vast and well-thought-out theology first taught by Jesus himself, who distinctly transformed the exclusive teachings and beliefs as propagated by the Jewish hierarchy into the inclusive and life-affirming good news that *all* are welcome in the 'kindom' of God.

For this reason, I was delighted when the Archbishop of the Anglican Church of Southern Africa asked me to join the Commission on Human Sexuality – tasked to engage with Anglicans across southern African and recommend ways in which the church could embrace and minister to the needs of those within the LGBTQIA+ community. It was a massive task which, like most church commissions and committees, raised more questions than it answered, and uncovered more uncertainty and hesitancy within the leadership (especially among the bishops) than it provided clarity or comfort to those in need.

Just as we had argued that to attach the label 'black' to someone and use it as a means of discrimination and oppression, so too was it wrong to use the labels 'lesbian', 'gay' and 'bisexual' to deny those choosing to identify with them access to all the sacraments of the church, including marriage. But the decision-makers couldn't make this connection. The same church, so significantly a part of liberating the label 'black', continues to oppress, reject, ostracise and humiliate those who use the labels 'lesbian', 'gay', 'bisexual', 'trans', 'queer', 'intersex', 'asexual' and other more subtle but important categories being named within the spectrum of human sexuality. What we don't see is that these labels, when liberated from their past oppressive connotations, are stepping stones for individuals on their journeys to liberating their original faces. Similarly, when the label 'heterosexual' has been liberated from its positon of power and privilege, it can also be used en route to the discovery of an original face. We are not our labels, but they are a significant part of our journeys of self-discovery.

For a lesbian woman living in some parts of the world, not least in a South African township, her label is both life-giving and life-threatening. The strategic partnerships the label could elicit may fill her life with joyful and meaningful relationships, but used in the context of homophobic chauvinism it could be ominously dangerous and even end her life. Surely, for this reason alone, if no other, the church (for God's sake) should be a place of safety in which people can explore and share their labels, and find allies in the struggle for full liberation? Surely the church should be a community of original faces – a place in which people live and share in the joyful process of awakening to their true-selves.

And so it was that the Anglican Commission on Human Sexuality began its work setting up hearings across many dioceses, seeking to hear the stories of those who felt excluded on the basis of their sexuality or sexual orientation or preference. In the months of listening to agonising stories of rejection and humiliation, one story moved me deeply and best illustrates the urgency of this liberation within our society and the church:

One Saturday morning, we listened intently as a mother told us of her baby's first months of life.

What she described was a journey of pain and confusion. No-one, she said sadly, seemed able to walk the path with her – not the doctors, nurses, social workers, neighbours or, when it came to it, the clergy or parishioners of the church to which she belonged. Her baby had been born with uncertain genital sexual identity. On the basis of the baby's genitalia, this precious little one didn't fit into the neat categories of 'male' or 'female'. Doctors advised that, possibly around the age of ten, the child would self-identify as male or female, and maybe then some medical intervention would be an option.

Registering the little one's birth was the next trauma. Birth certificates make no provision for a baby whose genitalia cannot be used to determine a sexual designation. Then the baptism: 'Are you presenting a boy or a girl?' demanded the priest. Alongside these specific traumatic experiences were the general confusion and alienation the mother experienced in the wider community. *'Where is God?'* she cried. *'Did God give me this? Why was I given such a little child? Is God punishing me?'*

We are learning more and more about 'intersex'. It is one of the categories on the human sexuality spectrum – the 'I' in LGBTQIA+. Such children are no longer being 'hidden' in our families. We need to affirm our deep conviction that every person is made in God's image and carries their original face: a unique and beautiful face that they will want to wear one day with joy and pride.

We listened to that mother's story and sought to provide her with the assurance that the church, at least, will be a safe haven for her little one, and will be there to support and nourish her child on the journey they must undertake. That was three years ago. The church rejected the Commissions' recommendations and still has no mechanism for embracing this little one or understanding the nature of their sexuality. No mother should experience shame, guilt, confusion or loneliness.

No teenager should contemplate suicide because they're too afraid to own their sexual identity. No person must live 'in exile', in the confusion of an unembraced sexual identity.

Reflecting on the cruelty of the organisation of which I have been a part for over fifty-five years (since my confirmation as a boy), a church I represented while on the Commission, and a church whose trivialisation of human sexuality constitutes a brazen act of inhumanity, I sought to find words the dear mother could share about her beautiful baby. Maybe I'm being too hard on the institution of the formal church?

But in these situations, I'm reminded of the label used, I believe, to define those who stood and watched but did nothing as Jewish people were being dragged off to their death in concentration camps. They were called 'bystanders' – onlookers, unmoved, cold-hearted, maybe frightened spectators. Given the nature of the One the church follows and hails as its model, nothing could be more un-Christlike than being a bystander as a mother cries in confusion…

A Mother's Cry

Are they not all ours, these tiny-winged ones
come to rest in our arms,
lent to us for safekeeping, for setting free;
that they may unfold, grow in awe of us, we whose love,
undiminished by their awkward flights, crying nights,
their need for warmth, to be breast-held, beheld,
heralded as the angels that they are, come from afar,
to journey here, embodied souls, become one of us,
are they not our beloved children from God?

A Mother's Cry

Then why don't you answer me?
Did God not give me this one, to hold and love?
My third child you will not let me name –
not the same, you say.
Well, is a child not one whose eyes
delight to shine the light within, the light of God?
These lips against my breast, do they not drink a mother's love?
Do these hands I'm holding, not need filling?
These ears, do they not long to hear of the hope, I spoke
from the moment I believed God had blessed me
with this one you won't let me baptise as one come from God.

Well, this I say to you;
This one, this one, you call *intersex*,
is not second best,
but is the precious, beloved, highly favoured one
God blessed me with this year!

Owning my Otherness

Owning My Otherness

My own journey into otherness – to a deeper and more human acceptance of the many sides, aspects, and dimensions of our common humanity – is not unusual, but like all journeys, interesting. It was a sacred awakening brought about by a profound personal encounter. Several years ago, on 13 August, our second child was born. Unexpectedly (there were no clues during what seemed to be a normal pregnancy) she was born with Down's syndrome. Over 40% of children born with Down's syndrome have congenital heart conditions and our daughter died at the age of seven from complications following heart surgery. Some surgery, as we know, doesn't work.

But here, I'd like to reflect on the day of her birth. I vividly recall the sense that our world had crashed when we were told that our beautiful little baby had Down's syndrome. The news crushed us. The immense grief lingered for a long, long time. Not only had we now to embrace a 'handicapped' or 'disabled' child, as she was labelled in those days (today, I prefer the designation 'specially-abled'), but we also had to let go of many dreams we had for her. We were, after all, 'a normal family', expected to produce 'normal offspring'! Our children were expected to be smart, beautiful and successful; to make something of their lives, to play sport, to read widely, and be good citizens. They would graduate from university and take up positions in their field of expertise. They would be professionals, adding value to society, be happily married and create beautiful homes in which happy grandchildren would be born. They would believe sufficiently in God to be spiritual and in justice to be democrats. They would travel and understand the complexity of cultural diversity and cosmopolitan societies. They may even speak several languages. They would certainly make us proud!

Then suddenly, in the early hours of that morning, Anna was born and none of the above would apply. It simply couldn't. Our family had become 'abnormal' – different, marked forever. I was shattered. In saying all of this, however, I speak for myself. Although Jacqui and I shared so many feelings in the weeks that followed Anna's birth, Jacqui saw everything through a mother's heart and never doubted that her new-born child was special. Very special.

It took me several years to understand just how special Anna was and how exceptional was the gift she brought to us. Looking back now, I recognise and deeply appreciate the role she played in my transformation, in my growth, in shaping and forming me. Forever.

I was born into a weird and skewed society. Besides apartheid's inhumane and race-based policies that devastated South Africa, destroying the fabric of our communal soul, the country I grew up in was characterised by several concomitant features, especially patriarchal chauvinist heteronormativity. I choose this particular constellation of words, this poisoned phrase, because they best explain the world in which I was socialised. The context in which I grew up was definitively patriarchal. In truth, the Caucasian patriarchy dominated everything; school, church, clubs, the movies, books, university, parliament – all of these displayed white men as superior, at the pinnacle. Jesus, like Superman, was also white. My world was essentially chauvinist. My white South African maleness was intrinsically better than any other – and especially better than any femaleness – simply because it had been so ordained (by God).

As for the heteronormativity of it all, I am pained when I recall the inhumane homophobia openly displayed at my (whites only, boys only) school. To be anything other than a strong, successful, stoical, sexist heterosexual would be to become the laughing stock of six hundred boys – a fate worse than death for a teenager growing up in my world. Today we have the phrase 'toxic masculinity' to describe the culture of such a school.

I went to this school for twelve years and, year in and year out, overtly and covertly, implicitly and explicitly, subliminally and intentionally, the messaging droned on and on. It was also called Christian National Education. We absorbed it all. It defined our normal, and to be abnormal would be to step into an unredeemable otherness. One would rather die than go there.

We dared not even contemplate being other, for imagine the horror of being labelled queer. The humiliation of not being normal was more than most could endure. Caucasian chauvinist heteronormativity wasn't considered a privilege; it was the Way, the Truth and our Life, as Jesus himself had said.

I was fortunate to have a father who had narrowly escaped persecution by the Nazis and so was awake to the evil of Caucasian superiority parading as nationalism. I was also fortunate to attend a church (St George's Cathedral in Cape Town) where the Dean was, for over thirty years, a prophet of inclusivity, especially when it came to issues of race and sexuality.

I recall a leading and well-known couple at the Cathedral – Dennis and Bill – who were faithful partners and lovers crossing not only the divides of sexuality, but also of race. So the seeds of my cognitive dissonance were sown. Although I was force-fed one set of beliefs at school, at home and at church a more humane and inclusive foundation was being laid.

But nothing crumbled the vestiges of my Caucasian chauvinist heteronormative world like the birth of Anna. In a flash, the bone of my bone, the blood of my blood, my very own child, placed into my arms immediately after birth, was and forever would be 'abnormal'. There, powerless, with her exquisite blue slanting eyes and stubby fingers, she looked at me, took my hand and led me into the land of otherness. From now on, she whispered, an other, me, you call Anna (which means 'gift') has taken up residence at your hearth, in your heart.

I wept, and often have since. She did it with such love – such innocent and magnificent, enduring love. Nothing can compare.

She taught me that the world wasn't normal. Normality is a construct, a plot set by the empire to rid itself of discomfort. Abnormality is glorious, is freedom. She opened the darkness of my fearful attachment to normality and showed me the joy, wonder and love to be found in difference. She taught me that real love is the coming together of every little piece of otherness in one glorious wholeness. She showed me that we were made for togetherness, for union in our difference. She showed me the gentle, accepting face of God who loves beyond the visible, past the façades, whose love reaches deep inside and liberates our original face from the prison of normality. I was the handicapped one being freed from the callipers of my upbringing.

I pray regularly for the exorcism of the spirit of patriarchal chauvinist heteronormativity and its toxic masculinity that infests the souls of so many men. I give myself to be led by the spirit of Anna and all like her into the land of otherness – where in the light of the truth, we joyfully embrace and celebrate all that we are – made, as we are told, in the liberating image of a Great Other!

Land of Otherness

You led me one day – that blessed, broken, bonded-forever,
change-my-life day of your birth
into a land of otherness, holding
my hand, my eyes blinded by superiority,
the false reality, I once called home, then
you tipped the scales, your stubby touch, your unreserved smile
your I-love-you embrace about my neck, your mineral-blue eyes
steered me into a cosmos filled with forms and shapes
all belonging as One, but seen only by those who enter in, who
are broken open, turned inside out,
set free from normality, and
even when you left me here, adrift, bereft, in tears
I learnt it's where we're meant to be, one family
in this land of otherness, where
I miss you so much.

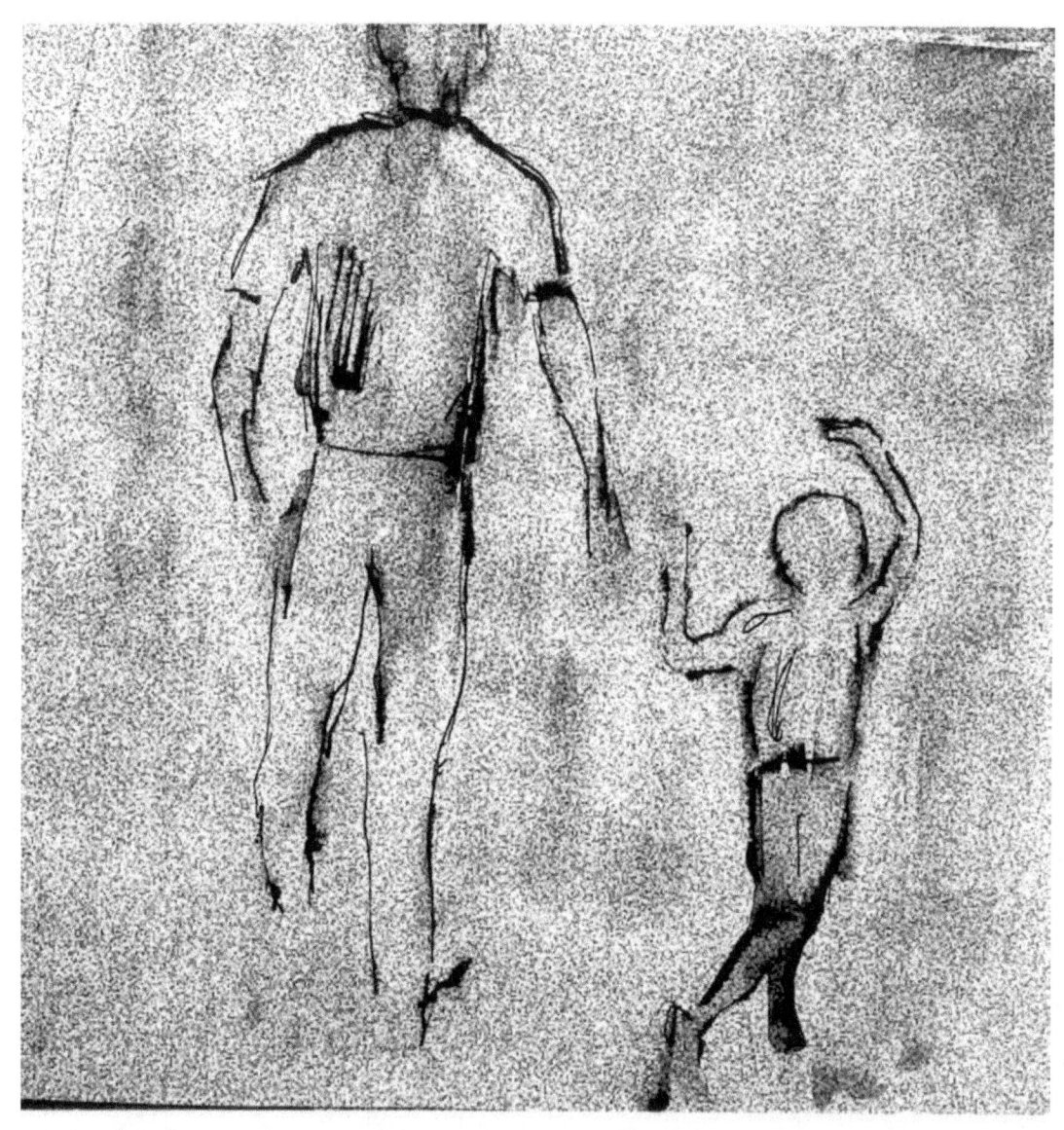

(into) the hand of otherness

This Family of Otherness in which All Belong

One of the lessons we who parent special needs children learn is that there is a family out there in which we belong. It is universal, cross-cultural and profoundly special, and filled with astonishing people who have and are navigating deep waters. The land of otherness is a place of hidden heroes who daily manifest the triumph of the human spirit. These are the unseen ones, without whom our world would be unquestionably diminished and because of whom the world is unquestionably enriched. These are the ones who know first-hand that suffering can break you apart, pain can kill and grief can destroy, but also that when suffering, pain and grief are faced, engaged, and worked with, they can be transformed into big-hearted compassion.

I have met many wonderful people who have manged to cross the fjord of pain and suffering and emerge as heroes, champions, saints, or what in Mahayna Buddhism is known as a *bodhisattva* – a person who is able to reach nirvana but delays doing so in order to bring compassion to the suffering. This surely must be the definition for love – that one who has come to the gates of fulfilment, joy and peace, voluntarily turns away and chooses to go on bearing the cup of compassion to those in need. Such are the ethics of those in the land of otherness.

Friends of mine, Neil and Jenny, are among those who have journeyed in this land. Their courageous story of compassion and fortitude is centred on their first-born son, Guy, who came into the world with one of the most infectious and beautiful smiles ever seen, but also with severe cerebral palsy that would confine him to a wheelchair and round-the-clock care for forty-four years. He died on 22 January 2021. The path on which he led his beloved and devoted parents, and later his two brothers, weaved its way through many deep, dark, difficult valleys of desolation and into fields of sweet consolation (as St Ignatius named them). It was never easy, but never a burden. Neil and Jenny bore their cup with pride and humility, without any awareness of the physical borders of this land, which is so characteristic of the citizens of the land of otherness.

At Guy's funeral, surrounded by thirty special needs adults and their carers – all dear friends – his mom and dad and brothers planted a tree. Amidst tears and laughter, grief and wonder, we stood in silence, overcome by what this beautiful child-become-man had brought into the world. What doors had he opened in those he touched? What tenderness had he called forth in those who cared for him? What world did he enter and what world did he leave behind? For it wasn't the same.

Ode to Guy

Could suffering ever be redemptive?
Can any sense be made of it?
Could his life, in some mysterious way
be a sacrament,
an outward sign of an inward love,
that blossoms in the ground
of every being,
even in the desert?

Could his presence have ushered in
a realm of which we're unaware,
too deaf to hear?
Could his grey-blue piercing eyes
be holding back our stormy skies?

Could his palsied body be the binding
on our broken world?
Could his courageous spirit be a bridge
across our lonely cries?

Could his bursting smile, his heart-felt laugh,
his slender hands, his lanky limbs,
his presence in the world,
often-times filled with pain,
but lived without complaint,
be a model, that by its contrast,
to the way we live, in the end

be pointing to a freedom
we have yet to comprehend?

And even as we let you go, dear Guy,
your ashes rooted deep within,
we wonder at your tender sacramental love,
which even through the layers of complexity,
was always free.

Redeeming Suffering

Can suffering ever be redemptive? Can we find meaning in what we can't understand? These are among the philosophical inquiries great minds like Plato, Aquinas, Augustine, Confucius, Lao Tzu, Kierkegaard, C.S. Lewis, W.E.B. Du Bois, and many others have sought to answer over the years.

While they may provide important insights into the great answers, what I have experienced during my time as a pastor and therapist is this: that in the end, helping people come to terms with *how* to deal with things, is more important to them than seeking answers as to *why*. How will we endure? How will this shape us? How will I live without her or them? These are the pastoral questions to which, in my experience, we can find answers.

To the anguished mom who asked if God gave her his child, my theology can provide long, complicated and unsatisfying answers. I can try to explain the God as one who doesn't hand out certain kinds of children; we can talk about the doctrine of freedom of choice that seeks to explain why bad things happen to good people; we can teach about a love that will make all things new and about an eschatological hope that won't disappoint. But this seldom helps. Rather, what would help her is the compassionate acceptance of her beautiful little babe into a community of *original faces* who, like her, are journeying in the land of otherness. Here she may find answers to how best to cope, how to ensure that her little one grows up with every advantage and without fear or humiliation. Here, she will be embraced, loved and set free from the curse of normality.

God in a body

Long ago, I read the following sublime insight shared by author, pastor and progressive theologian, Nadia Bolz-Weber. It speaks so powerfully to the mom at the Commission hearing and to each of us.

> *So I guess what I am saying is to hell with shame. Damn the shame about wanting sex or the shame of not really wanting sex at all. Damn the shame about being in a sexless marriage. Damn the shame about pleasure itself. Damn the shame about the harm done to us. And for sure damn all that shame about our bodies.*
>
> *For you carry in your queer, straight, cis, trans, fluid, fat, thin, short, tall, hairy, disabled, beautiful body the very image of your creator who has claimed and named you as their own. That voice is the voice of* love. *And it is eternal. And no other voice – not society's, not the church's, not your family's – and certainly not the snake – gets to tell you who you are.*
>
> *Shameless* (2019)

Epilogue

I have sought to share some initial thoughts on labels and their complex nature – on how they can become gateways into the glorious land of otherness, but that they can also be abused and turned into dangerous weapons of hate.

For all who experience oppressive othering, for all who have been liberated by their own otherness, and for those, like me, led into the land of otherness by a visiting angel, let us live by this extraordinary statement of the truth, immortalised by activist Rosa Parks and quoted frequently by one of Africa's great statespersons, Robert Sobukwe: *'There is only one race. The human race.'*

But I reserve the last words for Erika Trafton, from a beautifully vulnerable letter to a community magazine about her own child:

> *'Am I gorgeous?' my child asks …. 'Yes,' I say, 'You are.' … Pudgy fingers decorated with pink polish trace sequins on the bodice [of a pink and teal dress] … Little feet dance in sparkly red slippers. 'I'm just like a real princess!' 'Yes,' I say, 'You are.' …*
>
> *This child, my son. He is four years old and prefers to wear dresses. Maybe it is a phase, maybe not. Even as I wonder how I produced such an angelic-looking creature, I wish he would put on some pants and go back to playing with toy tractors – not because it matters to me (it doesn't) – but because I am already hearing in my head the name-calling he will face in kindergarten. Many adults already seem a bit disturbed by the dresses. Strangers utter awkward apologies when they realize he's not female … This culture has no room for little boys who want to be gorgeous. He picks up a parasol a neighbour gave him and opens it jauntily over his shoulder. 'Am I beautiful?' he asks.*
>
> *I sweep him into my arms and plant a kiss on his cheek. 'Always.'*

The Sun magazine (September 2010)

The Broken Teeth of Failure

Endings are new beginnings

ALMOST INEVITABLY, our ideally ordered universe – our 'private salvation project' as Thomas Merton called it – will eventually disappoint us, at least if we are honest. At some point in our lives, we will be deeply disappointed by what we were originally taught, by where our choices have led us, or by the seemingly random tragedies that take place in all our lives. There will be a death, a disease, a disruption to our normal way of thinking or being in the world. It is necessary if any real growth is to occur.

Richard Rohr, 'Disorder: Stage Two of a Three-Part Journey' (2020)

In the previous chapter, I wrote about the arrival of our daughter, Anna, born with Down's syndrome. Her arrival was shrouded in grief, and it took me years to understand the miracle she was – the gift I didn't deserve and then, too soon, couldn't hold onto. Interestingly, I never experienced

The House I could not Build!

her birth as a failure. No, Anna was no failure – she was a magnificent and victorious expression of life, grace, liberation, inclusion, wonder, mystery, joy and love. She steered me home to the land of otherness from which I shall never return.

Before saying something about my personal experience of failure, I want to recognise those whose sense of failure may be accompanied by pain, grief, and the death of a loved one.

My experience was relatively minor, and it may even appear as an exaggeration when compared to others. But there is a relativity in these things and for me, this experience was huge! The failure that ended my ideally ordered universe was not unlike that experienced by many people, especially entrepreneurs.

The House I could not Build

About eighteen years into my ministry – around the time in life when one begins a defining project, a new and exciting job, celebrates a major appointment, or begins to achieve long-held ambitions – I left the full-time parish-based ministry to become director of the Desmond Tutu Peace Centre. The dream was to build a legacy centre in honour of Desmond Tutu for whom I had worked as chaplain some years earlier.

After five years as Tutu's personal chaplain – during the fraught, last and dreadful years of apartheid – I went on a three-month sabbatical. I spent most of the time in the USA exploring museums, community centres, presidential libraries, grand memorial sites, and dreaming up what a Peace Centre would look like in the new democratic South Africa. I was particularly moved by the Holocaust museums that have been established around the USA and in many other parts of the world. The United States Holocaust Memorial Museum in Washington DC was an overwhelming experience.

Nine years later, with the Arch retired from the church and steering the Truth and Reconciliation Commission – the time had come for the Peace Centre to be established. Some of his former staff set up a trust, a funding entity, and I was mandated as trust director to manage the process of establishing the centre. What an extraordinary opportunity!

Seven years in, I resigned, defeated. (Today, the Peace Trust has been incorporated into the Desmond and Leah Tutu Legacy Foundation.)

The vision was to build a Peace Centre based on the visitor-attraction centres I had seen in many part of the world. Nothing like this existed in southern Africa at that time, so we were on virgin ground. The Peace Centre would be moving, singularly distinctive, so that every visitor would be irrevocably challenged and moved by spending time within its walls and exhibitions. It would be a 'must visit' when in Cape Town.

Based on the essence of Tutu's own moral philosophy and theological beliefs, the Centre would be a repository not so much of politically inspired stories, but of stories shaped by the contextual spirituality that had moulded his life. The Centre would distinguish itself from an apartheid museum (there wasn't one at that time, but obviously one would be coming) by focusing on the those who had fought for freedom from within the context of faith – like Martin Luther King, Óscar Romero, Sojourner Truth, Simone de Beauvoir, William Wilberforce, and Mahatma Gandhi, and especially those like Helen Joseph, Lilian Ngoyi, Albert Luthuli, Beyers Naudé, Denis Hurley, Albert Nolan, Oliver and Adelaide Tambo – all of whom came into the struggle as a result of their faith community and upbringing.

In addition, we could tell the world that it was Christians who had both dreamt up and defeated apartheid – that this soul-destroying crime-against-humanity political ideology had its roots in theology and was justified by Christian theologians on the one hand, while others, using the same Bible would find the theological justification to oppose and work, sometimes sacrificially, for its overthrow. The world could be a richer place as a result of this exploration – after, all, how else could we escape the truth that Crosby, Stills, Nash and Young sang in their song, *Cathedral*: 'So many people have died in the name of Christ / That I can't believe it all'?

The educational programmes, peace initiatives, civil-activist training and community development interventions would be rich and plenty, housed in an architecturally spectacular world-class design

that itself would provide visitors with a 'goosebumps experience'. I had visited the Guggenheims of the world, and the breath-taking Daniel Libeskind extension to the Jewish Museum Berlin in Germany, and come to understand that, in the modern world, these are the cathedrals or temples of experience. They are filled with numinosity and luminosity, much like one experiences in some special wilds
of nature or in great historic buildings like the Taj Mahal in India. What could be more thrilling than to be part of such a creative enterprise? It undoubtedly was a once-in-a-lifetime opportunity.

It nearly came together and much was achieved. We obtained a prestigious piece of land in the heart of Cape Town. We developed exhibition and building designs, did costings and compiled the requisite plans. We ran pilot programmes and consulted widely, setting up international partner organisations in the UK and the USA who would assist with ongoing sustainability. We ran workshops and focus groups, retreats and seminars. But, in the end, it wasn't to be as I had envisioned it. Breaking my teeth on a house I could not build was the most painful professional experience of my life.

I once thought I should submit a thesis titled *'How not to build a Peace Centre'*. I could give several insights into the issues one has to contend with in pioneering a start-up venture of this nature – maybe of any nature. While better qualified people have written much about these matters, if I were to list the most salient lessons learnt, they would be these…

One: There must be unanimous agreement around the vision. The vision is everything, but it is only achievable if all the significant players are unconditionally aligned and supportive. (With hindsight, I see this was never the case!)

Two: All the vision, dreaming and imagining in the world doesn't deliver a project if you don't have the core skills and competencies to pioneer, direct and manage such a process. (I simply didn't have them!)

Three: If you don't have the skills, surround yourself with those who do have them. (I frequently choose incorrectly!)

Four: Be bloody-minded. Don't be distracted from the core task, which is to operationalise the vision using the right people with the right skills. There are a lot of wolves dressed in sheep's clothing out there. (I'll not comment on some of the consultants we used!)

Five: Failure is sometimes the universe's way of saying 'No'. Imagine if the Peace Centre, once opened, had flopped? Other projects of this nature have. The timing was wrong. The buy-in from significant people wasn't there. The business model wasn't sustainable.

Six: There is no such thing as failure – just a time for deep reflection and the long, slow process of getting up again, as well as being open to the lessons you've learned. (I learned more about myself, God, meditation, forgiveness, healing, visioning, creativity, management and life-in-the-fast-lane through this project than from anything else in all my life.)

Seven: Know when to leave. Nigerian poet, Titilope Sonuga wrote the commanding poem *'10 Things (somebody should have taught me)'* – the second of which is *'Know when to leave'*. It continues, *'Some bridges need to be burned / Use the light to find a better way'*. Profound advice, indeed. I took it to heart and left, but the fire burned me.

I changed after that. My path veered off into a wilderness, where I slowly found my feet again and discovered new ways of envisioning the world, finding meaning in building relationships rather than centres, exploring the peace that lies locked in community living rather than in carefully crafted exhibits. Most importantly, I returned to a discipline I had started at seminary: cultivating a contemplative mind through daily meditation – a slower and more intentional open-heartedness to what *is*, rather than that which I want to force into being. This taught me the eighth lesson…

Eight: Creativity can't be forced. Lasting and profound creativity flows through us and not from us. The true creatives, I believe, are midwives or agents of something that wants to be born, of something bigger than themselves that comes from beyond, taking root deep within and then emerging. It was Maya Angelou who shared that when she was a young girl on her grandma's farm in the Deep South, one day, when out in the fields, she felt a poem beginning to arrive. Racing like a wild thing through the fields and gates, she reached the house and, grabbing a pencil and paper, made it to the dining room table just in time to write down the poem as it flowed through her. It would have been lost forever, she said, had she not managed to get to the table in time. Such is the nature of creativity.

Some years later, I found myself appointed rector at St Margaret's Anglican Church in Parow, Cape Town, where I experienced the happiest seven years of my entire ministry.

No Mud, No Lotus

Thích Nhất Hạnh –Vietnamese Thiền Buddhist monk, peace activist and magnificent human being – wrote a book titled *No Mud, No Lotus: The Art of Transforming Suffering*. I feel I really do know what he meant, but navigating the traumatic process or, to use Hanh's metaphor of allowing the lotus to emerge from the mud, takes time, patience, healing, love, and sometimes a good therapist.

As Richard Rohr commented, the nature of failure is a disruption to our ideally ordered universe, to our way of thinking and being in the world. It may, of course, bring with it much damage and pain, and we shouldn't trivialise its occurrence in someone's life. Yet it may mark the breaking open of the defensive clay shell we have used to mask the Golden Buddha within. Getting past the stages of anger, bargaining and denial, falling into the deep trough of introspection and working through the lessons, sets us on the path of awakening and emergence onto a new and higher plain as more authentic true-selves. In religious language, this can be described as the death and resurrection pattern.

In Christian imagery, the archetypal illustration is revealed in the person of Jesus of Nazareth, who is crucified (the failure), dies (lets go), and is then resurrected (a sacred awakening on a higher plain). In the following poems, I try to express the truth of this process…

That We May Be One

Oh God, so much failure
    Let the darkness enclose you; it is I
How can I forget
    That my light may arise on your asking
What happened for so long…
    And you may find rest from your pain
Why my teeth have been broken
    And hope in your longing again
On that house I just could not build…
    So, turn from your time of despair
You saw how hard I tried
    I have seen your upturned hands
During all those wasted years
    Nothing occurs that I can't use
Ending in such emptiness
    For from nothing it was that I made you
But for my endless contradictions
    Using all you are for the good
Running so deep…
    So come, let my darkness enfold you
Bringing me to this place
    That we may be One.

Sacred Moments of Awakening

Let the gloom enfold you; it is I;
I, in whom your failures fade,
your dark-rimmed eyes end
their peering search; I,
in whom your heart,
broken on stones that
would not build the house
you longed so to build
may rest.

I am your surrender, everything;
Here, your breath,
a shallow passing breeze,
is freed from its loyal task, here
your calloused piercéd hands
lay down their bruising load.

Here, no tongue, no mindless thought,
no more tearful holding onto hope or
waiting for another word or future dream.
Here, your whole-life is laid open, drawn
into my enfolding darkness
complete, buried, lost
to be found
anew in me
at each sacred moment
of your awakening.

So let it go.
Let your life go.

Failures of Living

There are other failures with which we have to live. As ministers, pastors in a community to whom people turn with their pain and conflict, there are times when we have to face our helplessness. We fail our communities.

We fail the people who place their trust in us. Think, for example, of the numerous cases of sexual abuse perpetrated by clergy. This is failure on a grand scale requiring a grand reckoning!

There are other failures – not of such gross moral culpability, but of a pastoral nature – that are hard to cope with nonetheless.

The Anguish of a Woman named Cee

A woman, let's name her Cee, once came to see me. She wasn't a parishioner – just someone from a nearby suburb who had received my contact details from a friend.

After our first meeting, I sat for several hours, reflecting on the pain she carried, the sadness surrounding her, her sense of longing, and the many unrequited questions about life she held in her broken heart...

I sought to summarise our first meeting in a poem.

Anguish!

Anguish

She came to see me today,
living with such anguish
her story tore my heart...

She came to say, today
how hard it is, making with those around her,
relationships of any depth...
Pushing and pulling, she feels the forces
that try to make and break her;
so hard to find the way out...

She brought with her, today
such frailty below the anger; such pain that burns,
feeding the wounds, nowhere to go...

She came to say, today
she's so uncertain, this way or that;
What to do? There seems no path...

Pushing and pulling, she feels the forces
that try to make and break her;
so hard to find the way out...

She shared her suffering, today
jagged edges cutting through a childhood,
its love unknown, for which she longs...

So hard to share today, she says
the pain gagging in her throat, choking the words,
to describe her aching heart...

Living on the edge, she wonders;
is it wrong, to want a home, a space to call my own;
to find myself, alone, but free?

We talked an hour, today
agreed there's no one way; except to listen and hold,
with open hands what's in the room…

We said we'd meet again,
next week, maybe more, as journeying home
means journeying through it all; the loss, the grief, the pain…

We made no promises, today
just trust that there is a way;
to make her way out…

She shared her anguish, today
she made me think of mine, not far away;
from which I too am seeking a way home…

She didn't keep the next appointment, but some weeks later she called and asked to meet again. We did – a few times, until my training and experience taught me that there were deeper psychopathologies present that would best be held by a clinical psychologist.

So we began reflecting on what it would mean for her to enter into long-term help. Very gently, after much discussion, I provided her with the names of psychotherapists I trusted. She agreed to make contact and, after one last session, we parted.

I felt deeply the anguish and pain with which she lived. I saw her from time to time, sometimes at a mediation service we both attended and then at a seminar. She mentioned that she was seeing a therapist, albeit erratically. I encouraged her to remain in therapy. She said she found meditation helpful, although, like most things, it was hard to maintain.

About two years later, I received a phone call from a person introducing herself as Cee's sister. She told me that Cee had died. Among her belongings was a letter she had written to her family in which she tried to explain her heart-rending decision to take her own life. Also in the letter, was a request that I conduct her funeral.

The family weren't Anglican and by their own admission hadn't been in a church for several years. With the unequivocal support of the wonderful people of St Margaret's, Parow, we conducted a beautiful, serene and profoundly spiritual ceremony, carefully crafted in consultation with the family, filled with poetry, flowers, meditative music, reflections and pictures of the one they had lost, who sadly had never been able to feel the extent of their love. Into the hands and mercy of God we commended her spirit. In my view, the God in whose name and presence we gathered was there too, not answering the question of why Cee had ended her life, but giving us the grace to accept and honour her decision, hard as it was.

It seems to me that 'failure' is a word God really understands but isn't limited by. And it seems to me that a God of Love doesn't prevent failure, but is willing to engage with us in the process of walking through it – transforming it.

Failure to Listen

I've been awakened recently to a new insight, a new learning. Saying that someone has 'committed suicide' is inherently unhelpful and undesirable. The phrase comes from a time when, like a crime that gets committed, suicide was seen as an act of deviance, an aberration, even an offense.

The point illustrates the importance of language and of its evolution, which applies across many of the labels we use. It also emphasises the importance of listening.

A teacher at the school I attended – let's call him John – unknowingly nurtured my desire to write poetry way back in the 1970s. A few years after I left school, John, who had moved on to teach at a university, took his own life. A note was found alongside neatly folded clothing on a beach in the Eastern Cape; a day or so later, his body washed up on the beach. I've thought about him often. That this gentle, inspiring teacher, surrounded by a whole school (and later a university) of people had been unable to share, to cry out, to find a listening presence, has haunted me. How often does it occur? What does this loneliness feel like?

And so I offer to you, John – vulnerable soul, un-listened to soul – this poem in honour of your courage and as an inadequate but sincere apology for not being there for you. I hope that these words help to awaken us to others who may be walking a lonely, empty beach…

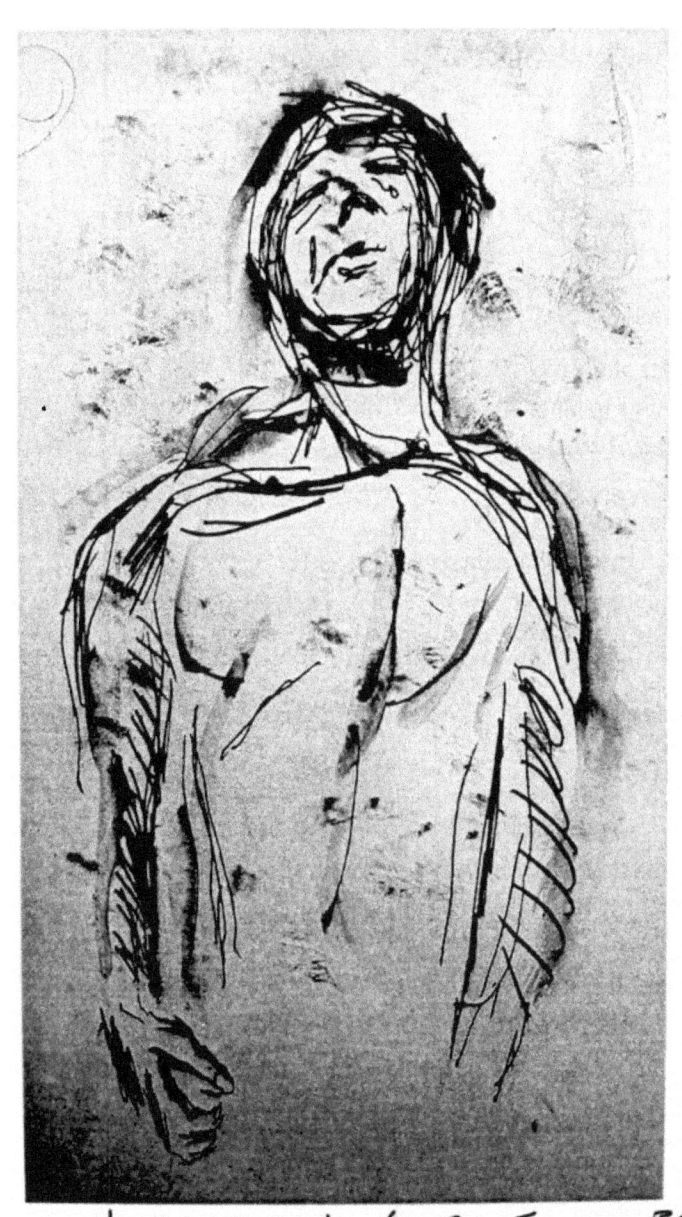

John Walker's Lonely Empty Beach

John's Lonely, Empty Beach

At the beach, on which I roam
alone, this fateful morning,
the wind rests from a passing storm;
Weary seagulls slumber aside the
seaweed, swept ashore, like the
flotsam of my mind,
thrashed by the tempest of the nightly ghosts
from whose release I come to plead
here, alone, on this lonely, empty beach.

Naked I embrace the dawning cold,
a welcome piercing of my salted, hardened heart;
Stumbling over crusty dunes
through tufts of tangled grass
which rise up like
my wind-blown thoughts, I
search once more, as before, for an exit
from this lonely, empty beach.

Then, the faintest sound, a
muffled symphony of spray,
then, from the waves, an emerging song,
a gong, an urging toll of chimes,
calling me to enter in
to a place of peace that lies, at last,
within my reach, off the shores of
this lonely, empty beach.

Hesitantly I offer first my hand,
and while cold to the touch, I feel
the waters clasp my waist;

And offering no resistance to its strong embrace
I commit this day to be my last
of combing through my shelléd past;
And while the numbing coldness
tangles with my breath
I celebrate the coming of my death,
which marks my thankful leaving
of this lonely, empty beach,
which has been my life of twenty-seven years.

The Balm of Lamentation

I end this chapter with a few thoughts on lamentation. The Bible contains a book of this name, which depicts the desolation of the tribe of Judah after the fall of their city, Jerusalem. The people wept, overwhelmed by the enormity of the tragedy; they grieved collectively, sharing their personal trauma communally. That is what lamentation enables and why it is a powerful tool in the grief-work toolbox of several cultures, especially those in which communal rites of passage and process remain intact.

There is much over which to lament today: the mindless destruction of our planet, violence, poverty, war, and the endless horror of loss that confronts so many people. Rites of lamentation, were they to exist in our fast-moving, emotionally sanitised world, would gather us together in events designed to evoke grief – allowing us to feel, to mourn, to grieve, and then to act. Communal lamenting is about owning our collective trauma, and accepting our accountability as well as our agency in taking action to address the causes. There are some non-profits that work in this space; the Institute for Healing of Memories, for one, does remarkable work around the world. We need to strengthen this work with faith communities and ministers who are trained and can enable such processes. Bob Geldof's Live Aid and some of the sets at U2 concerts come close to the kind of scale required to get the cold, cynical and secular-first world lamenting – awakened to the issues we're facing. We need processes that enable recognition, acceptance and ownership of our collective trauma. This is the necessary step before taking action, whether it be restitution, repentance, reconciliation or redistribution.

In our present world (notwithstanding the confines imposed by COVID-19), we frequently feel so far from community and the issues about which we should lament. We're so disjointed, so far apart from each other, so fragmented in our common life. There are ways, however, to engage in lamenting when isolated from others. Tibetan Buddhism teaches the powerful meditation practice *tonglen*, translated as 'giving and taking' or 'sending and receiving'.

To engage in *tonglen*, set aside a period of time and give yourself to lamenting a particular condition of the world. Choose a concern close to your heart. Find a still place and, sitting quietly, bring the concern to mind – let's say children dying from malnutrition in a refugee camp. Conjure a picture in your mind's eye that provokes a sense of urgency and empathy. Follow your breath: on the inhale take in the pain, hunger, desperation and anguish of the children (in this example), and on the exhale breathe compassion and healing on them. This isn't an act of masochism or self-immolation. Rather, it's about being willing to take your place as a world-citizen, a co-creator of the pain and so too of the healing.

With each breath, we offer ourselves, our own hearts so to speak, as the place of transformation. We become the agents of change. Thích Nhất Hạnh liked to say that those who engage in *tonglen* soon discover the path that leads from their cushion into the community. A meditation practice such as this is revolutionary, lighting within us the fire to change. 'And never diminish the power of one!' as Desmond Tutu always taught.

For those who want a Christian version of this practice, renowned Christian scholar, Neil Douglas-Klotz, in his work *Prayers of the Cosmos* (1990), suggests we can prayer by breathing in on the word 'longing' and breathing out on the word 'loving'. Thus we can prayerfully enter into the world of turmoil and trauma and be agents of God's loving transformation. I've been using these words in my own meditation practice, which I find deeply moving, connecting and empowering. I feel creation weeping in longing as I breathe in, and feel myself connecting with millions of concerned citizens when breathing out the loving that, for example, our planet requires. Of course I have to do more than just breathe love into the world, but this practice awakens me to the sacred tasks of social action and activism awaiting me after my morning practice.

It starts with the balm of lamentation – an agency-giving salve we all need time and time again.

※ ※ ※

The Balm of Lamentation

The Balm of Lamentation

In times of great sadness –
when children are fleeing,
clutching their parent's necks
in make-shift, sinking skiffs;

In times of great madness –
when leaders have abandoned us,
and integrity and honesty
die in dusty trenches of war;

In times of great suffering –
when a wounded child of strife
lives her entire life
in a grassless refugee camp;

In times of great grief –
when a beautiful daughter
just reaching her fullness
is diagnosed with a terminal illness;

In times of great bewilderment –
when churches close their doors,
deaf to the cries of a teen
who says I'm gay, queer or trans;

In times of great hypocrisy –
when voters abandon democracy,
choosing those who
shout racism and exclusion;

In these times –
when your heart is broken,
and you weep with every in-breath…
Then, know, you're being called
to a sacred awakening,
a setting free of humanity…
that'll take you from your
cushion into community
to begin again.

Epilogue

Spanish poet, Antonio Machado, knew about lamentation, which he conveyed in this poem:

The Wind, One Brilliant Day

The wind, one brilliant day, called
to my soul with an odor of jasmine.
'In return for the odor of my jasmine,
I'd like all the odor of your roses.'
'I have no roses; all the flowers
in my garden are dead.'
'Well then, I'll take the withered petals
and the yellow leaves and the waters of the fountain.'
The wind left. And I wept. And I said to myself:
'What have you done with the garden that was entrusted to you?'

What have we done with the garden entrusted to us? The unbearable question arises: What shall we do now? We weep and begin planting again.

Spiritual not Religious

Communities as wombs of awakening

■ ■ ■

ON ENTERING the little Boland village of McGregor, you'll come across a large, proud and dominant Dutch Reformed Church, sitting proudly in its walled plot – a formal place of religious worship representing a particular denomination of a particular religious faith. In the next road you'll discover, if you look carefully, a retreat centre called Temenos. Hidden behind trees, Temenos (from the Greek meaning 'sacred ground') is a place of peace and stillness – an inviting, gentle and distinctly spiritual place of rest and recreation. It seems to me that both the church and the retreat centre are metaphors illustrating a modern parable that explains the difference between religion and spirituality.

The church building represents religion. Walled and imposing, it speaks of an all-powerful God whose presence requires attention or at least respect. The gate is locked, except on certain occasions, and there was a time when entrance was governed by attributes such as race and membership. The architecture reflects a masculine understanding of God: bold, dominating, imposing, exclusive, and authoritarian. Within its walls, 'truth' has been taught to be about sin and judgement, about salvation and obedience, and about fires awaiting those who are not aboard. It is a place of compliance, of reformation based on moral systems outlined in coded testaments, lived out by the central religious figure of the faith: Jesus Christ. In this place, the ordained cleric teaches and the congregants listen.

The church belongs to a religious group with a long history reflecting a cultural journey over many years. It is governed by rules and regulations fashioned at synods managed largely by men. This church isn't alone. There are many like it across South Africa (and across the world), of different denominations and slightly different understandings, but together they reflect the institutional belief system called Christianity of just over two billion people.

Temenos, on the other hand, represents spirituality. It is soft, feminine, welcoming, with many openings – multiple gates, always open. On entering, you'll find many paths leading to many places to pause, to sit, to be quiet, recollect and experience. These places are diverse in nature and symbology – some reflecting the Christian tradition, while others are adorned with symbols sacred to Hinduism and Islam. In a corner garden sits a magnificent silent Buddha garlanded in prayer flags. Alongside you'll find 'The Well', a darkened chapel-like space in which silent prayer or meditation is encouraged and practiced. Candles burn and the scent of incense lingers gently in the air, embracing you without judgement. Here you are invited to awaken your senses. Peacocks parade their distinctive beauty while weaverbirds busily fashion their nests over ponds into which ducks waddle in peace.

Temenos is a place of enquiry, of curiosity – a place calling you to open up and to embrace all being presented to you. Here you can become still and know that Another is near. Here you can practice entering into the presence of God – however or whoever or whatever you may understand God to be. Awakening to nature, to a sense of Self, to something larger than your little self – this is the role of Temenos. Here the spirit is active – both the Great Spirit and your own. Here you can cry, learn, heal, dedicate, commit, accept, forgive, be forgiven. Temenos invites you into the world of the spirit, into an experience of love, where your spirituality is enriched by its practice. From here you can return to your daily busy life refreshed and awakened to the path that lies ahead.

■ ■ ■

Here's a poem I wrote during one of several retreats I've been able to have at Temenos…

Back to the Garden (of Temenos)

I sit in the garden and awaken
to a world I've forgotten
And know myself to be at home again at last
with One who has loved me
since time began;
And I soften
as the rain softens
the summer heat.

Back to the Garden of Temenos

I sit in the garden and know
this love to be my Source
my True-self, the lovely We,
the truest-me,
from which the green shoots,
the burbling brook,
the peacock's cry,
the busy bee and
the longing-me, all flow,
like scent that
fills the air.

I sit in the garden and feel
my heart, a rich bursting light
both mine and God's;
Filled with joy that not
the darkest of my shadows can dim;
This glowing heart within
that shines, ever-shining
here and beyond,
like the sun that greets
the morning sky.

I sit in the garden and delight
that I'm a channel,
though I'm nearly no one, nothing at all;
Just a chance, a once-off bloom
a morning breath,
but yet, by grace, a channel nonetheless
through which the Cosmos shows her love
day after day.

Which Comes First? Temenos or the Church?

Like all parables, this parable has its limitations. But it provides an entry point to the issues I explore in this chapter: the world of faith, the church, and Spirit; and a world filled by increasing numbers of young people who cry *'I'm spiritual, not religious'*.

From a western Christian point of view it certainly appears that, especially among young people, there is a deep longing for something spiritual, while at the same time a growing hesitancy to embrace formalised religion. Young people want to *experience* life and want their experience of religion to be a felt experience – something that touches and impacts their lives.

The crusty orthodoxy of mainstream churches increasingly doesn't cut it. as a result, many turn to the arm-waving, over-emotional charismatic churches that sadly only offer yet another form of placebo – a short-term psychic anaesthetic numbing the pain of the trauma in which many live.

Some become born-again religious fundamentalists, with God neatly boxed into a rule-driven life that provides all the answers to life's difficult questions.

Sadly, neither of these alternatives are sustainable and, within a few years, many young people burn out, becoming non-believers or at least cynical Christians looking elsewhere for authentic and trustworthy experience-based understandings of life.

As a result, many find their way into mindfulness, yoga and meditation, and other alternative spiritual modalities. They find meaning in vegetarianism, in championing social justice and ecological issues. They're willing to explore their sexuality without guilt and shame. They understand the importance of language, of moving the debates on. Many young people see justice not simply as a human rights matter, but also part of a larger struggle for freedom, which includes the liberation of the soul.

I once asked a retired bishop what he thought of this dilemma. He replied, surprisingly sagely, that the problem lies with the church persisting in telling young people who God is, while they are questioning who *they* are. 'We're not listening to the questions being asked of us', he concluded.

People and especially young people are asking questions about identity; about meaning and purpose; about relationships, education, sustainability, inclusion and acceptance; and about the future of the planet. These are to do with the issues they are experiencing daily, involving race, sexual identity, freedom, violence, and finding fulfilment in their lifetimes. Mainstream churches seldom raise these issues, or do so in the context of formalised dogmatic teachings removed from daily experience.

To return to two metaphors in the parable, I believe that young people (and maybe more congregants than we're willing to admit) are looking for a *Temenos-type experience* in their lives. But what we in the mainstream churches continue to offer is the old unchanging *Formalised Church-type experience* as illustrated by the Dutch Reformed Church standing so proudly in the town. I'm not referring, of course, to the actual Dutch Reformed Church *per se*, but to what it symbolises in the parable: a masculine, exclusive, authoritarian, rule-bound, male-dominated understanding of God. I want to suggest that it *is* possible for Christians, young and old, to have daily experiences of *Temenos* – to experience a vibrant and life-giving, non-judgemental, affirming and lasting spirituality.

Let's pause for a moment and recall how the parable described Temenos and, by definition, what we mean by saying we need daily *Temenos experiences*:

> *Temenos is a place of enquiry, of curiosity – a place calling you to open up and to embrace all being presented to you. Here you can become still and know that Another is near. Here you can practice entering into the presence of God – however or whoever or whatever you may understand God to be. Awakening to nature, to a sense of Self, to something larger than your little self – this is the role of Temenos. Here the spirit is active – both the Great Spirit and your own. Here you can cry, learn, heal, dedicate, commit, accept, forgive, be forgiven. Temenos invites you into the world of the spirit, into an experience of love, where your spirituality is enriched by its practice…*

I believe this *can* take place within the context of mainstream churches, within the context of formalised religious practice. But there will have to be significant change. The point is that we can bring *Temenos* into our daily lives and, more importantly, we can bring *Temenos* into our churches.

Bringing Temenos Into the Church

Over the years, I've been privileged to experience a variety of *Temenos type experiences* in the church.

One such example is the contemporary contemplative community of *Taizé* in France. It is a community filled with people who daily experience and practise a joyful, life-giving and relevant spirituality in the context of a religious framework that speaks to young people today. For me, my visits there have been life-changing experiences.

I've also been privileged to experience, in India, two religious communities practicing their spirituality in ways that are both deeply experiential and life-giving.

The first was during a visit to the motherhouse of the *Missionaries of Charity* and, for a few days, participating in some of their work in Kolkata. The second was a brief retreat spent at *Kurisumala Monastery*, an ashram in Vagamon. Here, fifteen monks (Catholic brothers) live high in the plantations, surrounded on their farm by several Indian families who, together with the brothers, farm the land and live a rich communal life.

Closer to home, I've also been very privileged to have witnessed first-hand a Christian leader who is deeply committed to orthodoxy and identified with formalised religion, but whose spirituality is palpable, real, visceral and relevant to the world in which he lives.

Desmond Tutu is able to make the church relevant – *'to make God accessible'* as my wife, Jacqui, once said. Tutu has managed to bring *Temenos* into religion. He practices a spirituality that enabled him to understand the concerns of ordinary people. His faith is both spiritual and religious, making both seem natural and real.

The community of Taizé, Mother Teresa's sisters of charity, the brothers of Kurisumala, and Desmond Tutu, are among a vast number of people who live in *Temenos* daily and bring into the world the fruits of their *sacred garden experience*

More Signs of Temenos

In this context and spirit, I want to again mention the people of the little *Anglican Parish of St Margaret* in Parow, Cape Town, who became a warm and welcoming family to Jacqui and me for the seven years I served there. Memory is kind and I may be guilty of a little embellishment, but at St Margaret's there truly was an attempt to live a more *Temenos-filled* church life. The Parish Vision spoke to this attempt.

Instead of a many-worded vision statement, we developed four pictures that became our common mantra, reminding us constantly of the kind of parish we sought to be.

First, we were *a church without walls,* which spoke to the deep desire to be inclusive – to be a warm, welcoming human family in which everyone belonged, regardless of history, belief system, race, age, sexual orientation, nationality or culture. What was important was that you felt at home.

Second, we were *a church swimming upstream,* which spoke to our desire to be counter-cultural, anti-hierarchy, non-conformist, and 'anti-empire', with its programmes of consumption that kill the imagination. Especially, we sought to swim against the patriarchal theology that dominates the church with its constant reference to God as a masculine figure. The appellation *'Father God'* was phased out. In our liturgies and prayers we sought to introduce inclusive language that spoke more to the immanence rather than the transcendence of God.

Third, we were *a church of wounded healers*: people living in a complex world, acknowledging our wounds and needs, but actively seeking healing – open to what Thomas Keating called 'The Divine Therapy' or the healing work that occurs when we open ourselves to the love of God. We did this through the introduction of meditative prayer, contemplative practices, and times of communal silence during our services.

Fourth, we were *a place of community* – a physical precinct that needed to serve our community needs. We needed a beautiful garden in which to pray and hold retreats; a beautiful sanctuary in the church in which to hold all manner of liturgies. I joked constantly about burning the pews in order to have seating arrangements more conducive to building relationships and a sense of community. We also needed a hall (the renovation of which is underway) in which to celebrate, to party, to hold receptions and wakes, workshops, courses and other community gatherings.

St Margaret's, Parow, was therefore *a church without walls, swimming upstream, filled with wounded healers in a place of community.*

I could never have hoped to have had a happier ending to my ministry as a parish priest. The seven years spent among the beautiful people of St Margaret's was a rare and real blessing!

■ ■ ■

Confessions of a Guilty Participant

It seems to me that much of mainstream church life is and always has been concerned about the church. So much of Christianity is about maintaining and running the church, and not about being Christian. We've turned our attention to keeping the institution going and lost sight of those for whom it exists. We've made the Sabbath more important than the humanity for which it was designed. We've lost sight of *Temenos* and spend an enormous amount of time worrying about how to preserve the large church building with its dominant spire. Much of this is caused by the absence of a vibrant, life-giving spirituality. There is insufficient *Temenos* in the church and those of us who lead and have held leadership positions in the church aren't sufficiently exposed to *Temenos-type experiences*. We can't give people what we don't have.

We need help. Without a deeply introspective exploration of our current model and way of being, mainstream churches are on a long, slow path to irrelevance. In offering this critique, I very much include myself.

I've been an Anglican priest for thirty-eight years and, while I've sought to raise my voice alongside those who have called out the church on its racism, its sexism and, more recently, its rejection of the LGBTQIA+ community, I too am guilty of worrying more about church buildings and their spires than about the people who gather within them. Moreover, it's because I love the organisation to which I have given my life that I feel eligible to critique it. I have benefitted enormously from my membership of the Anglican Church of Southern Africa and have found immense solace in my belonging. So, what follows are the confessions of a guilty participant – my critique and appreciation of the church that reflects a mixture of love for and frustration with it. In this context, I speak of the Anglican Church of Southern Africa.

The Church as Sepulchre, Tomb and Womb

While it may be that church leaders never set out to exclude or hurt others, and while it is true, as I have said above, that there are many remarkable people within the church and that grace abounds in a variety of church settings, we need to balance this by remembering how frequently the church, through its rules and decisions, has caused deep hurt. So many people have experienced rejection, whether by commission or omission.

Jesus' greatest criticism was of the religious leaders of his time; the ones with the responsibility to make known the love of God, but instead placed on their people the heavy burdens of religiosity. Jesus also once described the religious leaders of his time as 'whited sepulchres' – looking good from the outside, yet filled within with death. In this spirit of self-criticism, this poem seeks to illustrate the point…

This Blessed Church!

This Blessed Church, with
its Fathers in black and God in the clouds;
While our streets are strewn
with murder and pain, and

our pews filled with cries
of mothers whose daughters have died
at the hands of our brothers
whom we baptised.

This Blessed Church, you
ask me to love by observing the laws;
While the ones over there
whom we can't hear, for
we're so busy in church
deep in our prayer
asking God to keep safe
those *we* hold dear.

This Blessed Church, its
bishops in copes, rings on their fingers;
Knowing what's best
but failing the test
of hearing the cries,
of those on the edge
asking a question,
about the latest rejection
of those who are different!

One Still Crying in the Wilderness

Sadly, among the many churches to be deaf to the cries of humanity, the Anglican Church both locally and universally has a long history of not answering the questions asked by those at the edge and who may appear different. Among the latest of these *'rejections of the questions'* was the response of the Anglican Church of Southern Africa to recommendations put to the 2019 Provincial Synod (the church's highest decision-making body) on the inclusion of the LGBTQIA+ community. The Anglican Church has refused to recognise gay marriage and, to date, has forbidden its clergy from performing such marriages or even blessing such ceremonies. The homophobia displayed by some members of the church, even at the Synod, was and remains tremendously cruel. What made this more disappointing, more painful, was that this was the same church that, under Desmond Tutu's leadership, had come out so forcibly against apartheid's abuse of human rights. Now, contesting yet another of the human rights desperately needing recognition, the same church turned its back.

Desmond Tutu's long and illustrious ministry in the church always reflected the best of Anglican values. His ministry marvellously mirrored the essential teachings of forward-thinking Anglican theology – a theology based on love, inclusion, forgiveness, acceptance, participation, justice and liberation. Tutu seemed infused with a daily experience of a God who cares for everyone on this planet and, indeed, for the planet too. This gave him the ability to see the specialness within every person. He longed and worked for a world in which every person counted and was able to share their special giftedness without fear – a world in which the colour of one's skin, one's gender, one's sexual orientation and 'not even the size of one's nose', he would add, could stop us, penalise us from being who we are. That's why he fought against the rabid racism of his time. That's why he fought for the ordination of women in the church. And that's why he's spoken out so clearly in favour of the full inclusion of the LGBTQIA+ community in the church, saying on one occasion, 'If God was homophobic, I'd rather go to the warmer place!'.

The sad truth is that Tutu and the church weren't aligned on this issue. When one of Tutu's daughters married her woman partner, the Bishops of the Anglican Church of Southern Africa disallowed him saying a prayer of blessing at the wedding ceremony. In an extraordinary twist of fate, the Anglican Bishops of the church Tutu had served with such dedication, distinction, loyalty and steadfast faith were able to do the one thing that the apartheid government had tried to do for years – to silence Desmond Tutu!

Here is my inadequate tribute to Desmond Tutu as well as my very inadequate recognition of all who have felt the church's rejected over many, many years – those *on the edge*, whose questions aren't heard or answered. To all who feel unheard by the church, especially the LGBTQIA+ community, please know that there is an Archbishop who has consistently sought to make a place for everyone in God's world...

The poem is distinctly imperfect and even a little childlike – exactly as, I believe, Tutu thinks of himself – imperfect and always chuckling at how odd it was that God should use him for such a task!

■ ■ ■

Still Crying in the Wilderness
(For Desmond Tutu on his 90th birthday)

Voice of the Voiceless, they called him;
Baptised Mpilo Desmond, a gift
from a poor teacher's home
in the Wes-Transvaal,
born in the midst of the Great Divide,
to become pastor to the people!

No future without forgiveness, he predicted;
But only after he had demanded,
'Let my people go!'
in the tradition of
Moses and Luthuli and King,
the Mahatma, Romero,
Ngoyi and Maathai,
to name but a few.

In silence he prayed, alone in the mornings,
through long dark nights,
(sometimes, for whole days),
recalling the names of those
in prison, and especially

the children whom he always
held close to his heart.

On the streets, he marched,
in protest and in song, carrying
the hopes of the wounded,
the youth and all who longed to
become We, the People.

At gravesides, he blessed
the fallen, whose bodies were broken
in cold cells without reason, and
on the streets of the townships
and even in the
back of police vans.

Loudly he proclaimed, from pulpits
and lecturns, that freedom is indivisible, and
'til all are free, none are free,
and for weak and strong,
Life is One,
in which all belong!

Over and over, he taught,
with his hands in the air, that
black and white, straight and gay
women and men, ordained and lay, that
local and foreigner, homeless and sojourner;
ALL are children made in the image
of the One God.

Down the street, he danced,
that bright day, when at last

Madiba walked past his prison gate,
on his release, saying:
I greet you in the name of peace!'

And then in the end,
he led a commission
for uncovering the past,
of some of the truths
so, at least a few mothers,
could know, at last, where
their beloveds lay buried.

But since that bold voice,
through age has grown silent,
few Words have been spoken,
and some ask, are the prophecies broken?
For voiceless seem those
who follow the path he
walked before them.

We look to the churches, and see
no outrage, no vigils, no fasting;
So little sharing by those who are wearing the
robes of compassion, while
children go begging, their
mothers are beaten, and
gogos use their pensions
to feed the five thousand.

Sadder still, from the synods we hear
a message so clear:
Gays may not marry;
Women shouldn't hurry, for

Men aren't quite ready to end
Patriarchy; and the Youth
should refrain from sex before marriage, which
is the domain of those who claim
heteronormativity.

Saying little of our beloved Mother Earth,
whose destruction and pillage in village
and forest…
Oh God, *senzenina*?

(Pause)

And while many wept, grieving the silence,
new voices emerged, shaking and breaking
the norms and the rules:
a girl-child fighting for eco-justice,
women overcoming femicide,
teenagers redefining sexual identity,
young adults reclaiming spirituality,
and even men reframing their masculinity…

Yes, the voices remain, though not quite the same,
but they're still pointing the way,
he's wanted us to go, on this,
his 90th birthday!

Breaking Out of the Sepulchre

The Japanese monk and poet, Ikkyū (1394–1481), bemoans in a poem:

> *Every day, priests minutely examine the Law*
> *And endlessly chant complicated sutras.*
> *Before doing that, though, they should learn*
> *How to read the love letters sent by the wind*
> *and rain, the snow and moon.*

Inspired by Ikkyū's words, and staying in self-criticism mode a little longer, this is my version:

Endless Love Letters

Each day, the priests recite their liturgies
filled with their beliefs and truths
Laying on their hearts so many ifs and don'ts.
Before starting their prayers, faithful as they may be
Should they not learn to read the love psalms
sent by the wind, the sun,
and see how even
the shadows reveal beauty?

■ ■ ■

Laying on their Hearts so many Ifs and Don'ts

Jesus reserved his greatest criticism for the religious leaders of his time (mostly the Pharisees) laying heavy burdens on the shoulders of their people, while not being willing to lift a finger to move them. He was, of course, referring to the ritualistic and dogmatic conditions laid upon believers by the priestly class, preventing them from experiencing the love of God.

Still today, one repeatedly hears Christian preachers laying on their [people's] hearts so many ifs and don'ts. If you will do this or that (usually repent or confess or accept), then God will love you. When did God's love become conditional? How is it that the entire salvation project depends on my puny consent? That isn't to say that I don't have agency, even responsibility in responding to God's love, but God doesn't stop loving me simply because I don't say the correct words at the right time! God knows the thoughts of my heart and they're far more articulate than the words of my lips.

■ ■ ■

The Church as a Womb in a Tea Plantation

Fortunately there are pockets of wonderful spiritual experiences to be appreciated, even while the mainstream church seems consumed by its religiosity. Kurisumala Monastery is a sacred garden, a portal into the spiritual, a place of renewal, and an answer to those who ask if it is possible find *Temenos* in the formal church.

Let me tell you about the time Jacqui and I visited this monastery...

> *The monastery is home to fifteen brothers – all monks of the Cistercian order, sworn to prayer and silence – a Christian ashram in the south of India. We are high in the tea plantations on the mountains that dominate this otherwise coastal state.*

It is amazingly beautiful here. The monsoon rain falls outside in downpours that flood the little lanes in a few minutes, leaving everything glittering in the sunshine. The monsoon is an experience in itself – a phenomenon to befriend; a saviour to this land of a billion-plus people, filling the dams and rivers and underground reservoirs for another year's worth of life, breaking the heat of the dry months, reminding one of the immensity and power of the Creator God who, as the psalmist says '…sends rain on the mountains from the heavenly home, and fills the earth with the fruit of your labour' (Ps 104).

Here in Kurisumala, in this little monastery, surrounded by the brothers in their saffron-coloured robes and barefoot, one is also reminded of the grace and gentleness of the Loving God who chose to live alongside humanity in vulnerability, sharing our load, our journeys, and even our death. As they go about their day, praying, working, cleaning, praying, preparing food and praying again – everything is done with intention, with simplicity and tenderness. I watch a brother preparing the altar for Mass.

Slowly and lovingly he lays the vessels on the table. Then the oil lamps are carefully lit; then the incense bowls and then the chains of freshly picked marigolds which edge the table; then the holy missal book. Each time he passes the aumbry (containing the Holy Communion), he pauses, genuflects, and acknowledges that God is here – the Unseen Presence in which we live and have our being. I realise that for this brother, laying the altar is not a chore, it is prayer. I'm reminded of the words of Brother Lawrence, a mystic and saint of another time, who said: 'God regards not the greatness of the work, but the love with which it is performed…'.

Here in the chair-less chapel, we sit in silence on humble mats on the floor. The silence is not a threat; it is not the absence of noise. Here, it is the means within which I may hear my own breathing soul, my beating heart and busy mind. In the silence, I slow down my compulsive imagination that seeks constant stimulation. I begin to sense a different rhythm; an ancient and earthy heartbeat that isn't mine but ours. In the stillness, I am unhurriedly but consciously nudged into releasing 'me' and become aware of the greater 'we' of community in which I live. What was it that Jesus said? '… When you pray, go into your inner room and shut the door and pray to your Father who is in secret…' (Matt 6). I realise, of course, that the inner room and closed door to which he refers is my heart, free of daily distractions and material desires.

Amidst clouds of incense and the ancient chants of Aum (Ōṁ), Shanti, Shanti, Shanti (Oh Love, Peace, Peace, Peace), I'm absorbed into a community much larger than the thirty devotees attending the service today. As I follow the Malayalam text in an English translation, I feel enchanted by the words the brothers pray and know that all is One:

> *Oh Formless Great Self, Blissful Intelligent Form, Destroyer of Ignorance;*
> *You are the Giver of Discernment;*
> *Dispeller of Darkness, You are the Giver of Light;*
> *Unborn and Eternal, You give us Pure Consciousness…*

And then, too soon, our stay at the ashram is over, and we are being sent off with the blessings of Brother Yesuadvan, who touches our heads with his hand as he blesses us in the name of the God he worships and about whom he and his brothers sang in the Mass just a little while earlier:

> *Aum – Shanti, Shanti, Shanti*
> *Aum – in adoration of the Self-existent One*
> *Aum – in adoration of the God-become human*
> *Aum – in adoration of the Holy Life-giving Spirit*
> *Aum – Peace, Peace, Peace!*
> *And may peace be upon everyone.*

■ ■ ■

The Church as a Womb in a Hospice

When I was at seminary, a friend and I wrote to Mother Teresa of Calcutta (now Saint Teresa of Kolkata) to offer our services as volunteers at her home for the dying. Although we had heard of this remarkable nun who was changing the world, serving the poorest of the poor in India, it was Malcom Muggeridge's exceptional book, *Something Beautiful for God*, which moved me deeply. It was his special description of her work at the Home for the Dying Destitutes – also known as Nimral Hriday or the Home of the Pure Heart – that grabbed me. I was mesmerised and committed myself to work there – one day. When Mother Teresa came to Cape Town in the late 1980s, I was privileged to meet her. She didn't disappoint; her presence was distinctive – a mixture of celebrity and deep humility.

When we decided to travel in India for the first time, my only request was that we visit Kolkata and spend some time at Mother Teresa's home and projects. By then, sadly, she had died, but at least I could see her tomb and maybe spend a moment praying there. And so it was that my desire and commitment made over forty years earlier came true. When we arrived at the motherhouse of the Missionaries of Charity in Kolkata to volunteer at any of the many projects the Sisters run, I was assigned to work at Nimral Hriday! This is my account of the church as a womb, a place of dying and living...

> *It was about thirty-seven degrees Celsius, with the humidity rising to ninety-three percent. Perspiration dripped as I entered the home for the dying and looked over the forty-seven male patients present that day. The nuns inspanned me quickly: 'Feed that patient lying in the corner', 'Help with this bedding', 'Help this patient back to bed', 'Turn on the fans', 'Wash the chai cups'. Then the main task was allocated to me: 'Feed Rahul', said Sister Mary Gillian.*
>
> *Rahul had been in an accident that left him with severe disabilities. He was unable to eat solid foods and needed assistance to drink his evening liquid meal – about a litre of warmed milk with additional nutriments. I pain-stakingly fed him, his large dark eyes watching my sweaty hand as it poured careful mouthfuls of warm milk into his toothless mouth. I called him by his name – aloud though softly. I knew he couldn't understand, but it seemed right.*

Looking at Rahul's ragged and scarred face, I tried to imagine that I was gazing at the face of God, whom the dear Mother liked to remind her followers is to be found in the faces of all humankind and especially the dying poor. I have to confess that I struggled to see Jesus there – wondering rather how it is that there seem to be so many Rahuls in the world? And what am I going to do about it? It was then that I saw the irony. In truth, it was Rahul who was 'seeing' the God in me – enlivening the voice of God in me; enabling me to feel the pain, the struggle and the plight of so many in the world.

And so we sat there, and for a moment we were brothers caught up in the simple act of eating – one brother holding the feeding cup, while the other gratefully received its contents. One in our common humanity. The God within each of us recognising the God in the other. Yet we were worlds apart – strangers from different planets – mine the planet of privilege and his the lonely planet of poverty.

Later, having left Rahul and his cohort sleeping at the Home of the Pure Heart, I made my way through the jostling streets of Kolkata where children bath in gutters of rainwater, old men drink masala chai, laughing teenagers walk home from school, and young men seek to sell their vast range of unsolicited merchandise, to the 'Mother House' where, in a simple chapel, Mother Teresa's unadorned tomb can be found. I sat next to her tomb for a long time, praying, seeking to hold all I had experienced – all that Nimral Hriday had given me; all that the speechless Rahul had said to me; all that had been awoken in me about poverty, power, service and commitment to justice and compassionate action in the world.

Sitting there, aware of this and especially of my feelings of profound powerlessness, I was deeply grateful to believe in a God who somehow makes sense of it all – a God who is the source of all life, who knows each and every life intimately, who holds Rahul and me in the palm of her hand, and who will bring all things to completion; a God who touched the heart of a young nun in India over seventy years ago and who continues to work through ordinary people like me and you to turn tombs into wombs.

The Church becoming a Womb

As a young priest in a large and very happy suburban parish, I was once accosted by an elderly parishioner (who generally showed immense compassion and love for her neighbour) who told me my problem was that I didn't have sufficient thirst for souls!

It stung sufficiently for me to remember this single line of criticism after all these years.

The truth is, I do indeed have a longing (thirst) for everyone to experience the love of God. It's a central reason I'm a priest. I believe in a God of Love – the Source – and all of life is an expression of love. God is love. In the beginning, love; in the end, love. Love imploding is the Christian version of the Big Bang. Love becoming incarnate is the central tenet of the Christian faith. Love drawing all creation into a loving relationship is our destiny. Love finding fulfilment is our adventure. Love finding meaning is our purpose. When I was about nine years old, I experienced this love on which my entire belief system has been built. Love is profoundly personal and entirely cosmic, universal. Helping everyone participate in love is the purpose of religion – its only reason for being.

Participating in love on a daily basis is what having a spiritual practice is about. Sharing love is the purpose of community. Nurturing love is our common vocation as human beings. Introducing people to love is the priestly work. Celebrating love is the essence of the church's work. But over the years, I've learnt that there are many ways of understanding this mysterious thing called love. I have many friends who don't share my view or who don't see the church as mediating love. Rather, many see the church as a guardian of love, closing it off to those who don't recite the correct formulae. Moreover, they say they can't understand the language the church uses when talking about love. We make it so complicated, shrouding it in religious concepts like original sin, atonement, a Father in Heaven, a devil in hell, a virgin birth, a Son of God become saviour… We do indeed make it very complicated.

One of the things my many non-church-going friends have done to humour me when we're together is to say grace before we start eating. More recently, we have been taking it in turns to say grace. One friend, not known for his religious affiliation, started his prayer by saying 'Lord Nature, we thank you for this food…'. I was a little overwhelmed by the beauty of the appellation he chose to address God –

whoever God may be for him. In my book, the God of love of whom I'm a priest would happily and lovingly appreciate that title.

I've learnt to be open to the many ways of describing love and to the many ways in which love makes itself known to us. The important thing is that we are awake to the influence of love – to feeling our need of it and our desire to participate in its sharing. I have a whole dictionary of religious language with which I can describe this love, its nature and work, but increasingly I'm agnostic about the language, wanting rather to focus on the experience of it.

Using as little official religious language as possible, I have put words into the mouths of apparent witnesses to the crucifixion…

The Faces of Good Friday: A Meditation

Judas, who betrayed him, speaks:

On the day he died,
we who watched were lost;
We saw no hope in this – this wasted life of promise
dashed like broken glass across our way.
All this love, joy and 'trust in me'
from one who in the end,
gave it all away
So meekly going to his death,
without a second look,
no thought of what he could have done
with just a word…

John, whom Jesus especially loved, speaks:

We'd seen him do it –
'Be still', he'd say to waves
and calm their torment;
The wind, he'd hush and fold away;
Of a 'kin-dom', he would speak
not here, not there, he'd say,
My kin-dom's of another world, another type
My kin-dom is within.
I thought I'd found it – when he kissed my feet at supper
with Mary Magdalene whom he also specially loved
I thought we'd found it then
this place of love within;
But now I look and it is gone…

Mary Magdalene, his dearest friend, speaks:

Standing here, the cold of death weaves us into one,
his mother and his friend and me;
The cold of death seeps also into him,
his bloodied beaten body held by nails onto the beams,
a body once held by me.
I see from time to time – fleeting images of why this had to be,
but can't keep them long enough to understand
the reason for this brutal death;
My love for him calls out for one last caress,
to hold him once again against my breast
as we had done on many cold nights before…

Mary, his mother, speaks:

The one for whom I sung *Magnificat*, is dying here before my eyes
The dream of all I kept within my heart is dying too,
as mothers know, who watch their children die too soon;
My soul mourns for him; O Lord
have you forgotten the lowliness of your handmaid?
Where is the strength of your arm?
Why scatter us, we of broken hearts?
Why put us down, we the ones you promised to exalt?
You have filled us with sadness and sent us empty away
Have mercy O Lord, have mercy!

Jesus, dying on the cross, speaks:

Today I say goodbye, dear friends;
too brief the years we've shared,
so few the lessons learned
though I've tried to tell you all I know;
Things beyond our reach, outside our grasp,

have come to make this day my last
for which I've long prepared; though you could not see
I feel you standing there watching me
and know your vigil at my side is soon to end,
for you cannot see that which I can see from here;
Though bent, broken, blinded, bleeding out,
I see a different world – beyond – but within my reach
And there awaits a love for all who pass this way,
a love that draws me ever closer to a light,
so much brighter than I've seen before
and into which we all will go...

Luke, a doctor who would later write a gospel, speaks:

By now it was noon,
the whole earth became dark;
And as a curtain hanging in the Temple,
split right down the middle, Jesus called out loudly,
'It is done', and breathed his last.

Church Beyond the Womb

The Resurrection is not only a huge mystery to those who believe in the full story of Jesus – his birth, his death, and his rising from the dead – but also a major stumbling block for most of my friends and maybe many of yours. To hold that Jesus was an enlightened soul is easy. To say he was the Messiah, 'the Anointed One', may make sense if you have a little knowledge of Judaism and understand the concept and role of a Messiah. But to say he was the Son of God, love incarnate, both God and Humankind in one, and that he overcame death and rose to become the Cosmic Christ is a hard ask, indeed! That's why it's called a faith. Another word for faith is trust. People of faith are those willing to trust the story as true (enough) to get by. Personally, I trust that God will understand my doubts and uncertainties, but I'm willing to believe in the big version of the story.

The Resurrection is Jesus' assertion that death is to be transformed not avoided; indeed, death is a prerequisite for transformation. Here's my attempt to capture the story of the Resurrection in approximately seven-hundred words…

■ ■ ■

The Resurrection

In the beginning, a shapeless void, all was still.
That first day an aeon ago.

In the tomb, a cold wrapped body, lying still;
the third day that Passover weekend.

Then a flutter, the holy breath
who a billion years before had breathed alive with a Word
a singularity in the dark
hovers again, seeking an entry-point
from which to open up the night;
to make again, a second dawn,
another, but different from the first.

Oh blessed ruach, gentle breath of the Holy Source
breathing life with a touchless touch, colouring all you pass,
filling silence with gentle chimes,
parting water, creating light,

passing now, this new dawn
through sealed door of stony tomb,
come again, to make anew, by finding there,
that cold and darkened day,
the buried One, laid there three days before.

The One they had crucified.
The One they called traitor,
a Danger to the State; who said he'd come
to give freedom to the poor and the favour of the Lord;
the One who kissed the leper's skin
and opened the eyes of the blind;
who had unlocked a child's tormented soul
returned a mother's only son;
asking only that they love each other, as, he claimed,
God loved them, and
that when they meet together
to eat the broken bread and bless the cup,
they remember him.

Later, some would recall, he taught
that by his death he'd take with him
death itself, in all its forms,
ending all enmity in all humanity
paying Karma's debt once for all
halting vengeance for all to see
reversing thus our cosmic fall...
And it was this, all of this, all of this,
that pinned him to the tree and now
like a heavy mantle, held him in the tomb.

For him the fluttering Breath had come again,
undetectable, imperceptible,

searching, seeking, weaving past rock and seal,
past guard and steel, seeping like the morning mist
into the tomb, towards the One lying cold within.
Just as a dove's downy feather floating to the ground,
it touches him – a Godlike kiss on lifeless cheek
rolling as does the morning dew, making moist the fragile stem,
dampening with new life the wrappings that enshrine his broken body,
penetrating the layers of his feeble frame,
tenderly restoring the body beaten so badly
on that brutal bruising Friday,
drawing closed the open wound
enlivening his torpid shape, forming in the tomb,
an eastern sky – the Easter sky – a crimson dawn
to break the barriers of death's dark night,
pouring light on the One forlorn.

And, as a lotus flower breaching through a muddy waterline,
like a mystic rose bursting forth in ripened bud;
like a celestial seed fusing in a cosmic womb –
new life ignites, there, in the silence of the vault;
at first, a tender gasp, then a beat, a stirring,
then the slow awakening,
a body birthing, a new unearthing
shrugging off the scarf of pain, pushing into life again,
for the first time, again!

It was whole-making,
a whole re-making right there and then;
One, wounded, broken, torn apart
becoming One whole in head, heart and soul.

And then there was light.
The first new day;

the cosmos rejoicing, angels crying
trumpets blasting birthing notes; as
flowing freely from his fingers
trails of burning cloth
reveal his love for all he now can hold again!

All he touches parts before him,
the rock like water rolls away;
What was closed is made to open
and he emerges into the day...
A rising sun, the Risen Son, the Human One
become the One Humanity.
A second Eden – a new Aeon –
no boundaries can contain the gift promised now for all
to live life fully, free of shadowed clouds
that hide The Way,
for the Risen One is the Risen Sun
filling all with light and life and love.

Shout to the world; proclaim each day
a grave became a manger
a tomb has become a womb,
one born a stranger, called Mary's son
has become Everyone – the Cosmic Christ,

in whom we live and breathe and find our being
in the never-ending dance, that began that morning
to embrace us all,
and will embrace us all,
and does embrace us all.
Amen

The Resurrection

A Womb of Love for Everyone

In my understanding of the Christian story – the Gospel as we call it – I'm entirely convinced by the doctrine held by many Christians known as universal inclusion or universal salvation. This doctrine teaches the notion of cosmic redemption – that God's love (made visible and human by Jesus) will ultimately reach every sentient being and, even more excitingly, all creation.

As an aside, there is a wonderful Jewish teaching that goes like this: Every blade of grass has its angel that bends over it and whispers 'Grow, grow'. Just as the angels are concerned about each blade of grass, they are concerned with you and me and every element of creation. The Christian scriptures are filled with promises of all things being drawn into the love of God.

Charles O'Donnell, a priest and one-time president of the University of Notre Dame, wrote the poem 'In the Upper Room', in which the disciple Peter asks John what he heard when he laid his head on Jesus' shoulder at the Last Supper. It's a beautiful poem that inspired me to imagine what it was that John heard. I adapted the opening stanza and was influenced by the overall theme and sentiment of O'Donnell's poem …

What did you hear?

What did you hear that night you laid, so close
your head upon his heart?
Did you hear him say a name?
Was it mine?

It was Peter asking the beloved one,
who after a while, slowly spoke:

I heard a heart weighing heavy in his chest
as though there were two worlds
being moulded into one;
I heard an anguished echo from beyond the clouds
I heard a voice accusing him of being wrong
I heard another urging him to carry on
I heard the gasp like one who'd seen too much
I heard tears welling-up from the deep
I heard a voice whispering 'yes' to death
I heard others question why
I also heard a mother's cry

And yes I heard a name, I heard a name
And it was yours, Peter, and it was mine
It was ours and it was theirs
It was every name of everything
he'd spoken into being at the start
All was named within his heart
I heard it all
so clear, so near
that night before he died.

It was Every Name of Everything

I started this chapter raising the cry of so many young people: that they are spiritual not religious. It is our, the Christian church's, exclusionary language and practices that drive people from our midst. As Christian leaders and clerics, it is our lack of participatory and experiential spirituality – our inability to offer a deep meaningful spiritual experience to our communities – that is at the heart of our shrinking congregations and their looking elsewhere to fulfil their spiritual longings. Yet we have a tremendous story to tell, and we have a mysterious and ever-deepening well of resources from which to draw. We have access to the very Source of life – the Breath of Creation. Our God of love knows the name of everything, and longs to be in relationship with everything, with everyone, without exception. Why do we make it so hard for everyone and everything to find this love?

A New Womb-like Church

Given that I've been critical of the church and its perceived hurtful and exclusionary behaviour, I should at least offer some ideas that could answer my criticism. I was deeply moved by some words written by the visionary Indian writer, Arundhati Roy:

> *What is this thing that has happened to us? It's a virus, yes. In and of itself it holds no moral brief. But it is definitely more than a virus. ... [It] has made the mighty kneel and brought the world to a halt like nothing else could. Our minds are still racing back and forth, longing for a return to 'normality', trying to stitch our future to our past and refusing to acknowledge the rupture. But the rupture exists. And in the midst of this terrible despair it offers us a chance to rethink the doomsday machine we have built for ourselves. Nothing could be worse than a return to normality. Historically, pandemics have forced humans to break with the past and imagine their world anew.*

This one is no different. It is a portal, a gateway between one world and the next. We can choose to walk through it, dragging the carcasses of our prejudice and hatred, our avarice, our data banks and dead ideas, our dead rivers and smoky skies behind us. Or we can walk through lightly, with little luggage, ready to imagine another world and ready to fight for it.

'The pandemic is a portal', *Financial Times* (3 April 2020)

In response, I wrote an article for a local newspaper titled **'Looking for a New Normal Church'**, in which I sought to offer my vision of a church enabled to respond to the crisis of our times.

Roy's article inspired many to reflect on the 'doomsday machine we have built for ourselves' and imagine something different. Is the virus opening a portal, a gateway between our old world and a new one waiting on the other side? Is the 'rupture' to which Roy refers deep enough to end the many undesirable aspects of the 'old normal'?

Graffiti splashed along a wall in Hong Kong suggested that we 'can't go back to normal, because normal IS the problem'. It certainly speaks to me, as does Roy's challenge that we 'can choose to walk through [the portal] dragging the carcasses of our prejudice and hatred, our avarice, our data banks and dead ideas, our dead rivers and smoky skies behind us. Or we can walk through lightly, with little luggage, ready to imagine another world'.

Spiritual writer Richard Rohr has reflected on the nature of liminality – the space between one stage and the next. To occupy a liminal space is to be on the threshold of a new era or phase. Are we living in such a space? Are we on the threshold of something new? Can we imagine it? Or are the forces that shape us – the lure of the 'me-first' world, the lust for more things, the longing for bigger barns – going to be too strong and corral us back onto the 'old-normal' doomsday machine?

How does all of this affect the church? Who is the church? In this instance, I refer to mainstream churches to which the majority of the world's more than two-billion Christians belong. More specifically, let's focus on the 'western' church as it is sometimes called. Roy's words challenge the church in as much as they challenge society as a whole. For the church, too, the pandemic presents an opportunity to decide what of the 'old-normal' should be left behind and what should be taken through the portal to a 'new-normal' church.

Here are some considerations...

First to be left behind must surely be the theology that has allowed the church to condone so much death? A lot of death has been condoned by Christians: the Crusades, the Inquisition, Holy Wars, burnings, slavery, colonialism, apartheid, genocides, institutionalised injustice, poverty, environmental degradation – so much of which has been practiced by Christians and endorsed by the church down the ages. Much of this deficient theology is rooted in the belief that God is vengeful and wrathful. A professor of theology recently told of her first encounter with God. It was in the lounge of her grandmother's home where 'God' hung on the wall in the form of a large oil painting depicting 'Him' as the (Masonic) All-Seeing Eye. 'He sees everything you do, my girl,' said her grandmother, the inference being clear: be good or be damned. The notion that God is 'up there', watching, judging, ready to strike, has plagued our theology, our lives and our self-esteem for generations. Deep in our unconscious, a message has been imprinted that all have sinned and fallen short. In a further twist of the obscene, not only is this God 'up there' and vengeful, he is a Father to be obeyed, clung to, embraced and loved! What comes to mind is the image of an abused child clinging onto their abusive father, hoping against hope that one day he will love them. Not only is this Father God intrinsically judgemental, he also has a special hatred for sinners such as homosexuals, immigrants, Muslims, protestors, Jews, capitalists, Communists – the list is endless. It's this kind of theology, the appalling misrepresentation of the nature of God, which has spawned hypocrisy, the abuse of power, the abuse of children and women, the practices of deceit, and exclusion within the church over decades.

Also to blame is the fundamental untruth that the church alone is the custodian of the truth – the only and infallible way to God. With this mistaken notion, let's leave behind the other fundamentalist dogma, especially penal substitution theory, biblical literalism, and the Second Coming, amongst others. But most importantly, let's leave behind the church's support of the patriarchy, with its gender-exclusive and gender-excluding roles, behaviours, rituals and traditions that have characterised the church since the fourth century. And along with the patriarchy would go the absurd titles, ranks and roles, most of which truly belong to an 'old-abnormal' church. Let's leave behind the titles, be it 'Your Grace', or 'My Lord', or 'Father', or whatever. Titles come not from anything Jesus or the early church taught, but from the kings and queens in whose courts the clergy served from around 350 CE onwards.

As a subset of the above, let's leave behind the masculine language used by the church to describe God. For too long we have heard of a *Father* God who saves *man*kind, and is the hope of *men,* and so on. The Persian poet Hafiz once said 'The words we speak become the house we live in.' Let's drop the language that perpetuates dominance, judgement and labelling.

Then there's the matter of the church's elitism and classism; its bourgeois status. The rot set in in the fourth century when Roman Emperor Constantine was 'converted' and turned the teachings of Jesus of Nazareth into middle-class normality. Before Constantine's profession of the faith, the church was filled with revolutionaries and mystics who mostly met in secret to share their radical belief in equality, freedom, sharing and compassion. After Constantine, as one of actor and writer Rainn Wilson's viral Tweets in 2019 described, 'The metamorphosis of Jesus Christ from a humble servant of the abject poor to a symbol that stands for gun rights, prosperity, theology, anti-science, limited government (that neglects the destitute) and fierce nationalism is truly the strangest transformation in human history'.

Finally, let's leave behind the church's archaic and outdated liturgies, furnishings and designs. I'm so ready to let go of *Hymns Ancient & Modern* and the over-sung evangelical choruses. And I'm ready to burn the pews and the plush theatre seats. And let's get beyond the fixation that the buildings are the church, and that it's only okay to use them on Sundays. My list of items includes a lot of prejudice, hatred, avarice, and dead ideas, but it's simply a starting point. The challenge will be for the church to let it all go, without becoming amnesic about its complicity in the history it helped to create.

What luggage will we carry through to the newly imagined church on the other side? Surely our imagination should turn to the way of life modelled by Jesus and so remarkably emulated by countless humble and unnamed followers over the centuries. Lives like theirs, empowered by a spirit of light and lightness, lived simply and in solidarity with the earth and those on the edge, are surely the templates on which to imagine a 'new-normal' church. In other words, let's not start with what doctrine or dogma we are going to carry through, but rather who are we going to emulate, be like, and how are we going to practice faith, not teach it? Imagine a church of people (not buildings) – a community of people who are spiritual, not religious; simple, not grasping; living in solidarity and not separate.

Is there a model that could assist us in this imagining? Re-examining the model of Christianity practiced by the early church would be helpful, but does it belong in the twenty-first century? What about a contemporary model that offers a new paradigm and structure for a sustainable and just future? One such model, coming not from ecclesiology but from economics, is Kate Raworth's 'Doughnut economics'. She calls for a new visual map and new metaphors to represent the future without compromising future generations. She wants us to move away from linear thinking – from the upward moving 'line of progress' ingrained in us all, to a regenerative and distributive model designed to engage everyone. She explains:

> *Humanity's 21st century challenge is to meet the needs of all within the means of the planet. In other words, to ensure that no one falls short on life's essentials (from food and housing to healthcare and political voice), while ensuring that collectively we do not overshoot our pressure on Earth's life-supporting systems, on which we fundamentally depend – such as a stable climate, fertile soils, and a protective ozone layer. The Doughnut of social and planetary boundaries is a playfully serious approach to framing that challenge, and it acts as a compass for human progress this century.*
>
> *https://www.kateraworth.com/doughnut/*

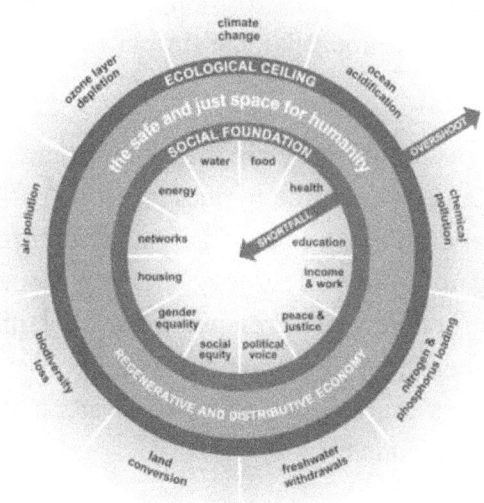

Raworth's Doughnut Economics Model (CC-BY-SA)

At the heart of the broken old-normal economic system is, according to Raworth, our fixation on growth as the single indicator of a successful economy, society or organisation. We need to replace the notion of 'growth' with that of 'thrive'. What do we have to do to ensure that humanity thrives? Raworth's model is so profoundly simple:

Doughnut economics draws two boundaries: an inner one we could call the 'human rights' boundary, and an outer planetary boundary. The model suggests that living outside of both the inner and outer boundaries is unsustainable and unjust. Staying between the two boundaries enables the planet and all people to thrive. It allows for growth, for diversity, and even for some self-interest, but it limits currently unfettered capitalism.

The model also suggests that the future is round not linear. The old-normal growth model is linear, rising higher and higher, driven along by the vectors of supply and demand. But we already know that, in ecological terms, supply can no longer match demand. A round system honours the earth's offerings, circulates resources, and values 'enough' instead of excess. It honours and works towards replacing the currently individualistic ego-systems with communal eco-systems.

How could this model challenge and change the church? For one, it would envision a church that is round, like the table around which Jesus gathered his loved ones, and the circle into which he invited strangers, sinners, doubters, non-believers, the marginalised and, in fact, everyone. Gone would be the pointy church; the old, hierarchical, pyramidal edifice – best illustrated by the absurd looking medieval pointed hats (mitres) worn by bishops – which we have learned can't simply be turned upside-down or, as some have suggested over the years, become round. Such a church would best be illustrated by small communities of equals meeting around a common table, sharing resources, and caring for each other as each has needs – just as the early church operated for the first three-hundred years of its life and before Constantine captured it. A church based on the model of Doughnut economics: round, thriving, inclusive, regenerative and distributive! How extraordinary. Just the word 'round' conjures a range of images:

looking for a New Normal (Round) Church

Round as in a mother's arms – inclusive and embracing. A round God, whose reach is wide and open, in whose embrace there is space for all. No-one need live in exile, as Tutu sought to teach us.

Round as in a model of leadership that is circulated, passed around according to gift and capacity, not title and privilege or gender.

Round as in always looking around for who may be left out and why?

Round as in solidarity with the planet – reusing, recycling, redistributing; making things go around so that all have enough.

Round as in a moral compass reminding us that how we sow is how we will reap; that what goes around comes around. Responsible and accountable, transparent and accessible.

Round in a relational way – describing the nature of conversation, listening, enquiry and reflection with people in one's immediate community as well as those beyond who also long to belong.

And most importantly: *round* as in centred. The middle of a circle is a still point – the place of centring prayer – where people gather for meditative, contemplative, rooted listening to the cries of the world, the weeping of the earth, and the healing whispers of God. Consciousness flourishes in this round spirituality, growing ever-bigger in diameter, ever-reaching outwards towards cosmic or Christ-consciousness.

A round church will be more concerned with getting everyone to live justly on planet Earth, and less so about getting people into heaven. In a round church, we look not up into the sky, but around at each other and, seeing God in every person, will want to ensure they're thriving. A round church enables relationships of mutuality, of intimacy, of belonging. In a round church, people see each other's faces and get to know each other's names. A round church doesn't need buildings. It needs carefully crafted spaces for communal gatherings that encourage personal and collective transformation – spaces that encourage people to thrive emotionally, spiritually and intellectually. A round church is encircled by larger 'rounds', and so enters readily into partnerships and alliances with all who seek to see the world thrive. A round church gathers around the urgent causes of the world, working with others to fight poverty, environmental destruction and inequality.

The model inspiring this new church is, by definition, flexible, soft, even bouncy. It is practice-based, not theologically driven. At its heart is the longing to see all thrive, and when one member isn't thriving, none can. It fulfils the law of love – to love God, neighbour and self; treating others as one would wish to be treated; and acknowledging that an injury to one is an injury to all.

The Doughnut economics model provides a raft of scientific and sociological theory that needs to be unpacked and applied to the 'round church' model. What measures are to be used to define the outer and inner circles of a round church? How will we know it is truly embracing the needs of its members? How will it apply the timeless and often elusive truths taught by its founder, Jesus of Nazareth? Who knows? But there is a portal and it's open now. When the pandemic is behind us, the lure of the shopping malls, the sound of the jet engines, and the treadmills of the high street will dominate our senses once again – and gone will be the opportunity to walk away from the carcasses of our dying religiosity and our polluted faith, and to imagine another church and be ready to love it.

※ ※ ※

Those of us who love the church long for it to be a womb: a place of birth, a life-giving and life-nurturing, richly blessed round space! We want to experience the God about whom we teach and in whose name we meet. We want our religion to be the source of love, not law. We want freedom to become, not conform. We want leaders inspired by their daily temenos experiences. We want prophecy, advocacy, pastoring and teaching that puts people first, and the church as institution last. We want the love that Jesus lived by. It is too much to ask?

※ ※ ※

Epilogue

I heard this story about a dying monastery from Jack Kornfield. Let its teaching be the last word for us...

Once upon a time there was a monastery that was slowly dying. No new novices were joining and the number of monks praying each day in silence became fewer and fewer, until only a handful were left.

One evening the monks met in council to discuss their plight. One monk, who had been in the monastery for many years, suggested that the Abbot visit an old Rabbi who lived alone in the forest nearby. So the next day, the Abbot walked the long forest path until he came to the Rabbi's hut. There, they greeted each other warmly and sat down to discuss their heart's concerns: the poor state of the world and the failure of their efforts to bring love to those in need, or to make an impact on the many issues facing the world at that time. Then the Abbot confessed to the real reason for his visit:

'I come to ask for advice, dear Rabbi,' he said. 'Our monastery is dying for lack of new members...'

There was a long pause, after which the Rabbi replied slowly that, strange as it may seem, he had had a dream just that night in which he had seen the Messiah in the monastery – alive and well and waiting to be discovered. After that the two men fell silent, meditating on what had been shared.

The Abbot returned to the monastery and shared the Rabbi's strange dream with his brothers. At first they were puzzled, wondering what this could mean and where the Messiah could be? How was the Messiah awaiting discovery? Where could the Messiah be hiding? Was he 'hiding' within one of them, as one of them? Was the Messiah hiding within the Abbot himself, they wondered? Surely not, for he would have revealed himself by now?

Was the Messiah within Brother Matthew maybe? He showed such compassion, especially towards those who felt lost. Was the Messiah maybe Brother Luke, with his deep understanding of theology and prayer and holiness? Or maybe, was the Messiah hiding within Brother Barnabas, who cared for the sick and who had seemed to appear in different places at the same time? Or was Brother Michael possibly the Messiah in hiding, even though he seemed a little impatient with those who read the liturgy incorrectly? Or was it possible, thought the monks when alone at their prayers, that each one could be the Messiah, but hadn't awoken to the reality? And so it was that the brothers became conscious that the Messiah could be in any one of them.

Over time, things began to change. They viewed each other a little differently, and treated each other with the deep respect and dignity – just as one would were one to engage the Messiah! They became more patient with each other, listened more carefully to each other, cared for each other, worried about each other's pains and nursed each other's wounds – emotional and physical, treating each other with the gentle worthiness with which the Messiah had treated his disciples. Indeed, how their worship changed, resembling more and more the last supper over which the Lord had presided. How tenderly they broke the bread and shared the cup with each other. And how they prayed – just as Jesus did – frequently and for long hours at a time.

Slowly, the monks noticed that people from the local village began picnicking again on the monastery lawns, as had been tradition. The locals in turn noticed that a great gentleness and kindness, a sense of welcome and community, had arisen among the brothers. They said it was love. They could feel it coming from the monastery, just as their parents had felt it in years of old. Young people began asking the monks about their life in community and if they could join in their daily prayer times. New vocations began to occur and many new novices joined the monastery.

Some years later, the monastery filling up with new vision and purpose and new vocations, the monks invited the forest-dwelling Rabbi for tea. 'Tell us once more about the dream,' they begged the Rabbi, showing their deep gratitude for his help in saving the monastery.

With a twinkle in his eye, the Rabbi replied: 'Well what can I say? All I did was tell your beloved Abbot that, in my dream, I had seen the Messiah alive and well and living here in your monastery – and by the looks of it he is!'

Journeying in the Desert of Love

Trust your heart – it knows the way

■ ■ ■

ON THE BULLETIN BOARD in the front hall of the hospital where I work, there appeared an announcement. 'Yeshi Dhonden,' it read, 'will make rounds at six o'clock on the morning of June 10.' The particulars were then given followed by a notation: 'Yeshi Dhonden is Personal Physician to the Dalai Lama.' I am not so leathery a sceptic that I would knowingly ignore an emissary from the gods. Not only might such sang-froid be inimical to one's earthly well-being, it could take care of eternity as well. Thus, on the morning of June 10, I join the clutch of whitecoats waiting in the small conference room adjacent to the ward selected for the rounds. The air in the room is heavy with ill-concealed dubiety and suspicion of bamboozlement. At precisely six o'clock, he materializes, a short, golden, barrelly man dressed in a sleeveless robe of saffron and maroon. His scalp is shaven, and the only visible hair is a scanty black line above each hooded eye.

He bows in greeting while his young interpreter makes the introduction. Yeshi Dhonden, we are told, will examine a patient selected by a member of the staff. The diagnosis is as unknown to Yeshi Dhonden as it is to us. The examination of the patient will take place in our presence, after which we will reconvene in the conference room where Yeshi Dhonden will discuss the case. We are further informed that for the past two hours Yeshi Dhonden has purified himself by bathing, fasting, and prayer. I, having breakfasted well, performed only the most desultory of ablutions, and given no thought at all to my soul, glance furtively at my fellows. Suddenly, we seem a soiled, uncouth lot.

The patient had been awakened early and told that she was to be examined by a foreign doctor, and had been asked to produce a fresh specimen of urine, so when we enter her room, the woman shows no surprise. She has long ago taken on that mixture of compliance and resignation that is the facies of chronic illness. This was to be but another in an endless series of tests and examinations. Yeshi Dhonden steps to the bedside while the rest stand apart, watching. For a long time he gazes at the woman, favoring no part of her body with his eyes, but seeming to fix his glance at a place just above her supine form. I, too, study her. No physical sign nor obvious symptom gives a clue to the nature of her disease. At last he takes her hand, raising it in both of his own.

Now he bends over the bed in a kind of crouching stance, his head drawn down in the collar of his robe. His eyes are closed as he feels for her pulse. In a moment he has found the spot, and for the next half hour he remains thus, suspended above the patient like some exotic golden bird with folded wings, holding the pulse of the woman beneath his fingers, cradling her hand in his. All the power of the man seems to have been drawn down into this one purpose. It is palpation of the pulse raised to the state of ritual. From the foot of the bed, where I stand, it is as though he and the patient have entered a special place of isolation, of apartness, about which a vacancy hovers, and across which no violation is possible. After a moment the woman rests back upon her pillow. From time to time, she raises her head to look at the strange figure above her, then sinks back once more. I cannot see their hands joined in a correspondence that is exclusive, intimate, his fingertips receiving the voice of her sick body through the rhythm and throb she offers at her wrist. All at once I am envious – not of him, not of Yeshi Dhonden for his gift of beauty and holiness, but of her. I want to be held like that, touched so, received. And I know that I, who have palpated a hundred thousand pulses, have not felt a single one.

At last Yeshi Dhonden straightens, gently places the woman's hand upon the bed, and steps back. The interpreter produces a small wooden bowl and two sticks. Yeshi Dhonden pours a portion of the urine specimen into the bowl, and proceeds to whip the liquid with the two sticks. This he does for several minutes until a foam is raised. Then, bowing above the bowl, he inhales the odour three times. He sets down the bowl and turns to leave. All this while, he has not uttered a single word. As he nears the door, the woman raises her head and calls out to

him in voice at once urgent and serene. 'Thank you, doctor,' she says, and touches with her other hand the place he had held on her wrist, as though to recapture something that had visited there. Yeshi Dhonden turns back for a moment to gaze at her, then steps into the corridor. Rounds are at an end.

We are seated once more in the conference room. Yeshi Dhonden speaks now for the first time, in soft Tibetan sounds that I have never heard before. He has barely begun when the young interpreter begins to translate, the two voices continuing in tandem – a bilingual fugue, the one chasing the other. It is like the chanting of monks.

He speaks of winds coursing through the body of the woman, currents that break against barriers, eddying. These vortices are in her blood, he says. The last spendings of an imperfect heart. Between the chambers of her heart, long, long before she was born, a wind had come and blown open a deep gate that must never be opened. Through it charge the full waters of her river, as the mountain stream cascades in the springtime, battering, knocking loose the land, and flooding her breath. Thus he speaks, and is silent. 'May we now have the diagnosis?' a professor asks. The host of these rounds, the man who knows, answers. 'Congenital heart disease,' he says. 'Interventricular septal defect (a hole in the wall between the left and right chambers of the heart) with resultant heart failure.'

A gateway in the heart, I think. That must not be opened. Through it charge the full waters that flood her breath. So! Here then is the doctor listening to the sounds of the body to which the rest of us are deaf. He is more than doctor. He is priest.

Richard Selzer, *Mortal Lessons: Notes on the Art of Surgery*

■ ■ ■

Journeying in the Desert of Love

Richard Selzer's exquisitely told story is beautiful for many reasons. It highlights so many important issues about which we could have many rich conversations. (As an aside, this story resonates deeply with Jacqui and me on a personal level. Our daughter, Anna, was born with an interventricular septal defect, among other heart complications. It was from the operation to repair the hole in the wall of her heart that she never regained consciousness – the *full waters of her river having finally flowed out.* Thus we have an understanding of the patient's plight). But the part of the story that speaks loudest to me are the words Selzer uses to end the piece: *So! Here then is the doctor listening to the sounds of the body to which the rest of us are deaf. He is more than doctor. He is priest.*

What we hear and see, touch and taste, is not necessarily everyone's reality. I say this as someone who, like most of us, has grown up in an era of rationalism, in which facts dominate, logic rules, things have to be proved to be true, and in which most things can be explained by the application of evidence. Anything else is considered suspicious if not superstitious, belonging to the Dark Ages.

In the time of COVID-19, let me immediately make it clear that I'm certainly on the side of science. I'm also on the side of medicine and its remarkable contribution to understanding disease and providing healing options. I'm also on the side of engineering and mathematics and biology, and regard the evidence being presented today on climate-change, for example, is true, accurate and dramatic. But I'm a believer. I believe in God and I can't prove it using the tools of modern rationalism. That's why Selzer's words move me so deeply. He accepts and describes so beautifully the way Yeshi Dhonden held two worlds together – with such *divine humanity,* if one may use such a phrase? Yeshi Dhonden is both physician and priest, moving seamlessly between what appears only to us as two worlds. For Yeshi Dhonden, I suggest there was no dualism, no two different worlds; the hospital was both a place of *science and of spirit*. To be able to discern the reality as he did and move within it, bringing truth, healing and understanding together in a unitive way – surely this is something to be valued, admired, sought after, loved and believed.

There is a way in which we can hold both rationality and belief – a non-dual or unitive way – but it requires some intentionality, a willingness to journey on a path that is only made by walking it. My experience of faith – *of the way* – started when I was nine years old. Since then I've had a consistent sense of being called, being held, and guided, and over fifty-five years of being transformed, ever so slowly. I've also realised that the journey is characterised by impermanence; each day is a departure.

There's a Way

There is a way and it's calling me
There is a hand and it's holding me
There is a light and it's guiding me
There is a love and it's transforming me

The walk of faith is made by walking it
There is no home; only
the daily arrival, and
the longing, and

Each day a departure on this Way.

Each Day a Departure on this Way

One night, in my tiny bedroom in my parent's home, I had a defining experience for a boy aged nine. Up until then, I had lived a pretty normal life – the youngest and fourth child of well-meaning, fairly formal Christian parents who attended a progressive Anglican Cathedral and faithfully said their daily prayers. After that evening, I continued to live a pretty normal life – so my experience was by no means a Marian Annunciation or a Damascus road epiphany, but it was very real and lasting, and stands out as a definitive starting point in my journey through the Desert of Love.

That night, as I lay in bed, having said a prayer (as my father had suggested), I had an experience of both light and love. Not dramatic, but distinct. A brightness seemed to envelop me, within which I felt a generalised in-pouring of love that was immediately trustworthy and faithful. It was focused on me, but not about me – as if I was being absorbed into it, while at the same time, I was absorbing it. I never doubted that the source of this love was God. This *was* God. God was light and love and, deep down, within the mystery of my boyhood naivety, there was a small piece of firm ground, unmoving and to which I could always return, and its name was love. Later, I would read how the wise, spiritual ones referred to God as the 'ground of being'. Somehow, I think I've always intuitively known what that means. Yet I never presumed my experience to be special or to make me special. Lucky, maybe, but not special.

I'm deeply grateful for this childhood experience for at least two reasons. First, it gave me a deep sense that love was right here, next to me, in me, and was unconditional. It lived all around me and most importantly, it lived within me. Later, I would learn that this understanding of God – to see God as being within everything – is described in theology as the 'immanent God'. Most western Christianity preaches about a 'transcendent God' – the God outside of everything, beyond us – God as a Father in heaven, for example. While this understanding of God is theologically correct, it is only partially correct. I have long been concerned that the over-emphasis on God's transcendence has closed the door on one of the most important journeys a Christian could ever make – what we could call 'the immanent journey': the journey inwards, down to the core of our being where we shall meet the God who lives within and who waits, longing to meet us on the inside, where our true-self lives.

The second reason I'm so grateful for that first and profound experience of light and love is that, around the age of ten, I had another visceral experience that had the power to shape my development. Not unlike many children, I went through a destabilising period that included sexual molestation. It wasn't lasting, but it was inappropriate and left its mark on my fragile psyche – a mark fortunately ameliorated by my earlier experience of light and love. Luckily, the ground of my being was never fully invaded and never overrun. There, in the midst of everything, in the midst of me, always, was the light and love – the ground of being to which I could return and remember my first experience. Of course there were times when my return to that inner ground was infrequent and erratic, but the light and love was never not there. Later, in times of anxiety, of loss, of bewilderment, the light gently revealed to me something deeper...

Oh Gentle Light

Oh gentle light within
so easily overshadowed
by my clumsy, flapping, endlessly-longing self,
you lead me to the inner ground
where you meet me in the silence

always revealing to me
the gentle source of love
which transforms
my clumsy, flapping, endless-longing
into my Deepest-me.

Journeying Deeper into the Desert

My boyhood experience of light and love marked the roots of my calling, my vocation. By the time I was thirteen, I knew I would one day become a priest. It was inevitable. I loved the thought of architecture, in the long tradition of the German side of my family. Medicine and clinical psychology were also options. But the priestly calling never disappeared.

During my late-teens and early university days, I held a special reverence for Thomas Becket, the twelfth-century saint who was murdered in the cathedral by his once-friend King Henry II.

Apparently, and as I understood it, Thomas and the young Henry were great friends and lived the high life, until Henry, wanting a loyal archbishop in Canterbury, expediently appointed Becket as Archbishop. The trouble was that, once Becket took the vows of priestly office, he became the model cleric – sober, chaste, devout and highly critical of the new king's outrageous lifestyle and politics. And so, one night, Henry's soldiers heard the king mutter the now infamous words, *'Will no one rid me of this troublesome priest?'*, whereupon they stole into the cathedral and assassinated the praying archbishop. My takeout from the story was that I could be like Becket and live the high life until my ordination vows would require me to become a model cleric. There was no point in being pious too soon! The time would come when I would be ordained and *then* I would take it all seriously. What has always remained with me, however, is the sense of God within – that the real road home was inward and downward, not outward and upward towards some abstracted God-in-the-sky.

Though written many years later, this little poem, inspired while on a retreat at Temenos, seeks to capture the sentiment that the way to love is within…

You Want to Find Love?

You want to find love?
Don' ask the waning moon where she lodges at night
nor seek for her in the silence of the holy places
or from those with scented veils;
Open, rather, the door of your heart,
kept locked so long
For there, she will enter in
but only then,
by invitation.

Encountering Ego in the Desert of Love

And so this has been my journey: inward and downward. Ironically, the more I was able to venture inward (assisted over time by an able and trustworthy psychotherapist and through years of spiritual direction), the more I was able to embrace the outer world with its complexity, diversity, urgent neediness and many demands. The deeper we go within, the more we're able to accept that which is around us. The more we find God on the inside, the more we see God in the world about us. The more we encounter the love of God within, the more we encounter the love of God in creation, in the world, and in others. It's a delicious irony, typical of the paradoxes found in the desert of love.

The Christian spiritual tradition is filled with references to the God within. Jesus preached earnestly about his kingdom being within us. As an aside, many feel it's no longer appropriate to keep referring to the 'kingdom of heaven'. Rather, it is suggested, we could use the term 'kin-dom', to emphasise its relational nature.

Many spiritual writers and traditions reference this understanding. Saint Hildegard von Bingen, a Germanic twelfth-century nun, mystic and healer, wrote in her book *Scivias*: *'You understand so little of what is around you because you do not use what is within you.'*

It seems she intuited the notion that the deeper we go *within*, the more we connect to all that is *beyond*. The more we are our true selves, the more we will reflect the cosmos. Psychoanalyst Carl Jung always found the words to bring spiritual and psychological truth together. *'Your vision will become clear only when you look into your own heart. Who looks outside, dreams; who looks inside, awakes'*, he once said. *'Listen to the wind, it talks. Listen to the silence, it speaks. Listen to your heart, it knows,'* is a saying from the wisdom of Native American peoples. *'Listen to your heart, it knows'* is a sentiment that one could spend an entire lifetime exploring and experiencing. *'Nothing is outside of you; your own kin[g]dom of fulfilment is within'*, writes Sarah Blondin, a modern meditation teacher.

And so began my journey inwards. Providing significant energy, fuelling it as it were, was a growing and abiding interest in meditation as taught by some extraordinarily appealing Christians like Anthony de Mello, Henri Nouwen, Thomas Merton, Thomas Keating, John Main, Richard Rohr, Cynthia Bourgeault, Brother Roger of Taize and, more lately, by Laurence Freeman, and the Buddhist teachers Jack Kornfield and Tara Brach. My practice was also hugely enriched by the example and direction I received from my magical spiritual director, beloved by many, Francis Cull. And of course, for the five years I was his chaplain, my spiritual awakening was deeply enriched by closely watching (and accompanying) Desmond Tutu. Tutu's commitment to daily meditation, or 'contemplative prayer' as he may call it, is sadly not sufficiently known or imitated by the clergy.

There are wonderful teachers of and books on meditation, as well as downloads and apps with hours of teaching and guiding. I once tried to write a series of articles – a sort of 'what-is-and-why' of meditation – but I said nothing that wasn't better said by others. The thing about meditation is that it shouldn't be talked about; it needs to be experienced. It's like learning to ride a bicycle – think how many lessons a child would stand before crying out: 'Stop talking about it and let me ride!'

Let me offer a few significant and beautiful quotations (among many) on what I am talking about.

The first is from the very wise and erudite Rowan Williams, a former Archbishop of Canterbury:

> *… contemplation is very far from being just one kind of thing that Christians do: it is the key to prayer, liturgy, art and ethics, the key to the essence of a renewed humanity that is capable of seeing the world and other subjects in the world with freedom – freedom from self-oriented, acquisitive habits and the distorted understanding that comes from them. To put it boldly, contemplation is the only ultimate answer to the unreal and insane world that our financial systems and our advertising culture and our chaotic and unexamined emotions encourage us to inhabit. To learn contemplative practice is to learn what we need so as to live truthfully and honestly and lovingly. It is a deeply revolutionary matter.*
>
> The Archbishop of Canterbury's Address to the Thirteenth Ordinary General Assembly, the Synod of Bishops (Oct 2012)

This second quotation, highlighting the revolutionary nature of meditation, is by Thomas Merton, who describes beautifully the awaiting realisation of one who meditates:

> *At the center of our being is a point of nothingness which is untouched by sin and by illusion, a point of pure truth, a point or spark which belongs entirely to God, which is never at our disposal, from which God disposes of our lives, which is inaccessible to the fantasies of our own mind or the brutalities of our own will. This little point of nothingness and of absolute poverty is the pure glory of God in us. It is so to speak [God's] name written in us, as our poverty, as our indigence, as our dependence, as our sonship [and daughtership]. It is like a pure diamond, blazing with the invisible light of heaven. It is in everybody, and if we could see it we would*
>
> *see these billions of points of light coming together in the face and blaze of a sun that would make all the darkness and cruelty of life vanish completely ... I have no program for this seeing. It is only given. But the gate of heaven is everywhere.*

Thomas Merton, Conjectures of a Guilty Bystander (1968)

A third remarkable set of insights comes from Julian of Norwich, the mystic and teacher of mysteries. She lived in the fourteenth century and wrote flowingly about her experiences of God in what has become known as 'The Showings'. With grateful thanks to Elizabeth Spearing for her translation of 'The Showings' and to John Newell for his remarkable summary of her visions, I have sought to weave a poem using Mother Julian's own words, phrases and understandings of God. I'm unhesitatingly a believer and follower of Mother Julian's God. I hope you could be too.

Mother Julian's God

O God our Mother and Father,
Womb of the Eternal
from whom we each have emerged;
We, the root stock of the One Essence,
not simply made by you O God
but made of you,
encountering you in our true depths.

As we know you, the One from whom we have come,
so we come to know ourselves,
for you O God, are the ground of our lives,
the essence of our being,
nature's substance, whom we swallow
and by whom we are swallowed
in the still waters of the earth.
O God, we feel you in our human bodies
and in the body of creation.
Your grace is given to save our nature,
not to save us from our nature.
It is given to free us from what we have become
and done to one another and to the earth.
Your grace, O God is given,
to bring nature back to that blessed point from which it came,
namely you, O God
It is given that we may hear again,
the deepest sounds within us, that
We are all One.

Mother Julian's God!

We have come from you O God as One,
and to you, O God we shall return as One.
And our lives are meant not for isolation but for relation.
For we, O God are the strands of time and eternity intertwined,
the human and the creaturely inseparably interrelated,
the One and the many forever married
the Soul of God and our many souls, tied
in an everlasting knot.

So help us O God, to hear
what is at the heart of the human soul
to listen to our deepest longings,
for the desire of the soul is the desire for you O God;

And while many of our desires
have become overlaid by distortions,
at the root of our being, O God,
is the sacred longing for union, and

the deeper we move within the human soul,
the closer we come to this divine yearning.
And the nearer we come to our true self,
the greater will be our longing for you, O God!
Our longing for you, O God!

What both Thomas Merton and Mother Julian capture well and hold out to us is the deep and sacred notion that within each of us there is *'a point of nothingness ... untouched ... by illusion, a point of pure truth ... inaccessible to the fantasies of our own mind or the brutalities of our own will. This little point of nothingness ... is like a pure diamond, blazing with the invisible light of heaven. It is in everybody...'*. If we add Mother Julian's understanding of the nature and location of God to Merton's noteworthy notion that within each of us is a *'pure diamond'* (and remember the story of the Golden Buddha covered with clay), we could say that at the root of our being is a pure diamond (or true-self) and the deepest longing of our pure-diamond nature (or true-self) is for union both with itself and with God.

The deeper we move within (or the closer we move to our diamond-self or true-self) the closer we come to God.

Another saint, Catherine of Genoa, said that this deep inner place, in which our true-self and God are one, is our 'Deepest-me'. It's a brilliantly clear insight. *'My Deepest-me is God'* – now *that's* something to meditate on for a long, long time.

Never mind finding God in the sky when you die, your Deepest-me is God, so why not go there to meet now and while you're alive?

■ ■ ■

The Inner-Me

As the holy ones have told us;
Within our longing
just below the heart;
there is to be found
the shimmering shape of
an immortal diamond, which is
both God and me...

Of which I know so little;
except, I feel the longing
see the shimmering, and
Sometimes, I hear a whispering…

'Within your longing,
your unrequited ache;
Look, can't you see
that the shimmering, immortal jewel
is God who *is* your Deepest-me?'

The Inner-me!

Isn't this is the gospel? In my view it is. This is what Jesus came to illustrate, to teach, to model – not only in words, but also in his life – modelling the pattern of how this all works! Jesus taught that within every person lies the kindom of God (the pure diamond or true-self, the golden Buddha, our Christ-nature or Buddha-nature – our real and authentic self).

Jesus once taught that a man discovered a pearl of inestimable value lying in a field. On discovering it, he went off to sell everything he had so he could buy the field (and, of course, the pearl!)

We are the field within which the pearl (or diamond) lies. Friends, if we have ears to hear, then we had better run and sell everything in order to buy the field. This discovery, rather than driving us into self-absorption and possessiveness, will bring us more into community – the joyful community of those who long for unity with others, with our sisters and brothers of other mothers, and with all creation.

Ironically, discovering our true-self, leads us to the true-other. And the true-other is every sister and brother out there waiting to become family. Even more wonderful, the true-other turns out to be everything in all creation. And so, in the words of one of St Francis' canticles, we too can call the sun and fire, brother; the moon and water, sister; and the earth, mother. Even death becomes a sibling.

At the heart of all of this profound experience, in truth, the vehicle waiting to transport us on this journey is meditation. It may be God's grace that motivates us and calls us towards our goal, but the vehicle able to carry us in and down, to convey to that point of nothingness, deep within is meditation or contemplation. As Williams said: 'To learn contemplative practice is to learn what we need so as to live truthfully and honestly and lovingly. It is a deeply revolutionary matter.'

And so it is to contemplation or meditation that we should turn daily. Here, using any number of techniques – and we can learn handsomely from other traditions, especially our Buddhist and Hindu family – we need to embrace the silence, the stillness, and become quiet, breathing gently upon our journey towards God and our true-self. This is the daily wonder and the daily grind: showing up, sitting, waiting patiently in the presence of God, for the Presence of God. As a teacher once told me, don't expect too much for the first fifty-nine minutes of every hour you meditate, and certainly don't tell anyone you meditate for at least the first twenty years!

I've sought to begin my day in this silence and, in developing this practice, Desmond Tutu has been the most significant influence. I watched him ensure that every day began in silent contemplation. If the working day was to start earlier, he simply started earlier. His sitting time was entirely non-negotiable. What a role model.

Daily Practice

On a trip to India, I arranged to stay behind in a temple we were visiting early one morning – knowing that if I left without having had my sitting time, I wouldn't find the time later in the day. I recall the temple with great affection...

The Temple, My Day Begun

Though the temple's empty,
I'm not alone, listening to the
fading sounds of worshippers departing,
muffled by the wind
in which one hears, some say,
the voice of One who visits
those who linger longer to pray here.

Outside, welcome sacred showers
wash the walls
with sacramental tenderness;
An outward sign of what
the seeker seeks within,
in the prayerful silence here.

Stillness calls me to the task
of being present to the One
beyond the noisy messy monkey-mind
every sitter longs to reach;
and so I sit.
A softened gaze helps me watch
the breath that enters in,
and with straightened back
I choose to let it go,

choosing, too, a deeper letting go
of all that holds me
separate and apart.

Thus the rhythms of this ancient art
begin their timeless work
and on the gracious tides of mindfulness,
sometimes
the Presence enters in
and for a time, (how long?)
we are One, all is one,
and then is gone;
my day begun.

We need to allow the rhythms of this ancient art to begin their timeless work. It's a quest, really, a daily quest – sometimes ending in sweetness, but not always. It teaches us not to look for the *path*, but rather, to patiently sit in the silence until the *way* finds us, which it will, in time…

My Sacred Quest

On my daily seeking healing sacred quest
I surrender
in hallowed stillness
peering for a path, and
finding none, I find
just a way
that leads me,
sometimes,
to the sweetness.

Journeying in the Desert of Love

Meditation calls us to recognise one of the most common default positions of the human mind or human condition: our need to control. Not a bad need when we are infants, for without our ability to demand our food intake, or get a nappy change, we could perish. We usually do this by wailing, crying out, to capture the attention of our caregiver. The matter of control becomes more complicated as we get older. Learning about self-control, delaying our need for gratification, and eventually our acceptance of death, are all lessons about holding on or controlling, as well as surrendering or letting go. The Buddha taught that our grasping, our attachment to all things including objects and life itself, is the single cause of suffering. Somewhere I've read, and I've often said, that our two base instincts are grasping and defending.

Daily meditation is sometimes called the *'practice of a little death'*. This isn't as grim as it sounds. It is an accurate reference to the letting go we need to practice in meditation. Sitting in stillness, stilling our minds' endless chatter by focusing on our breath or using a mantra, is to our ego-self a little like dying. That is why it resists the sitting. Meditation and its effect on the ego is a topic for much fuller discussion and, again, there are many wonderful teachers able to guide us in understanding and dealing with this complex notion. From my spiritual point of view, Eckhart Tolle, Richard Rohr and Thomas Keating are the wisest and most helpful. Essentially, though, while on our meditative journey, at some point – possibly daily – we'll encounter our ego.

What meditation teaches us that our true-self is wrapped in something akin to a hardened shell we can call ego. At first this is simply for survival – as infants and even toddlers we need this shell – but later it becomes a way of being that has to be undone, surrendered or died to. The core of the issue is that we confuse the necessary shell with a real self. It isn't. It's not real. It is, as some call it, a false self (just a shell) and not a self at all. That's why in the East, particularly, it is referred to as an illusion, unreal. We need to go deeper within, beyond the shell. We need the shell to crack open, to dissolve, to break down, so that the true-self, for which the shell was just the wrapping, can emerge.

This will be a life's work. Some call it a crucifixion. It is a death of sorts and many resist this dying, this giving up, this unwrapping of ego. Jesus explained this using a farming metaphor: Unless a seed is planted in the ground and dies, it cannot bring forth fruit. There's a dying required, a burial, a letting go, a surrender, a baptism – call it what we may – it's the path to adulthood and true-life, to the true-self. And it's at the heart of being free to be true.

There is no coming to consciousness without pain. People will do anything to avoid facing their own soul. As Carl Jung put it in his book *The Philosophical Tree*, *'One does not become enlightened by imagining figures of light, but by making the darkness conscious'*. As adults, what makes this unwrapping so difficult is that, over time, it becomes the locus, the storehouse of the memories of all sorts of hurts, grievances and trauma. Clinging to the wrapping, enshrining it, making it less penetrable, reflect the painful memories of our historical wounds. That's the darkness to which Carl Jung refers; elsewhere he calls it the shadow. In our shadow, we store all the introjected unpleasantness, all the negative material we have absorbed about our self. Again, the story of the clay encasing the golden Buddha is a valuable metaphor, as is Merton's notion of the pure diamond that lies within – both waiting to be found and exposed, enjoyed and shared with the world. We need to courageously and intentionally chip away at the shell that has been applied over the years by both ourselves and by others in order to find the golden Buddha, the pure diamond, the pearl of great value – all labels for our true-self which lies hidden within.

This is our work, our sacred work, to dive down beyond the surface and crack away the clay covering, unwrap the ego, and become who we are: vulnerable, human, open-hearted, authentic sisters and brothers of one family – the cosmic family – which includes every particle of creation. As First Nation elder, Black Elk, said: 'O Four Winds, help me walk the soft earth as a relative to all.' Richard Rohr calls this process the resolving of our inner contradictions. In one of his weekly summaries on the theme 'choosing life in the time of evil', Rohr encourages us to do this work: 'The people who hold the contradictions and resolve them in themselves are the saviours of the world. They are the only real agents of transformation, reconciliation, and newness.'

This, I do believe, is our work – our sacred awakening and our sacred work: to surrender to our Deepest-me, that meeting place a breath and beat away, where we are One.

Ode to my True-self

I feel you there, so close my heart
knows your presence
so close you are, just
a breath and beat away.

I know you hear me, see me,
this broken-shadowed-me
standing close; I move towards
your unchanging presence,
your shivering light guiding me, calling me
beckoning me, Come home!

I know that within you
lies my wholeness;
I know you to be the meeting place

between self and Source;
You, my connection, my point of reference;
I know you to be a place of acceptance,
of non-judgement, in which
I move and have my being;
Within your embrace, within you I live.

Your eternal commitment to me
unmoved by my shadow and bleeding-self
who sits beyond, outside…

attached to the many pictures and longings;
I know you to be holiness
the very heart of love
which is why
I'm so scared to enter in
and make my home with you…

Don't Be Afraid in the Desert

For those who love Sunday school stories, can you recall being told how many times in the Bible we are counselled not to be afraid? Some say there are 365 verses of this nature – one for each day of the year. Others say only 144. It doesn't really matter. Even Jesus suggests that we 'be not afraid' on several occasions. The truth is we are often afraid, and among the things we fear most is detachment or letting go, losing control and changing from one state to another. Death is the great detachment, the final letting go.

In the context of our spiritual journey, it is our ego that resists letting go. Ego is by definition a 'sticky' thing – clinging and grasping, resistant to change. In his beautiful poem, 'The Self Slaved', Patrick Kavanagh wrote:

> *Me I will throw away.*
> *Me sufficient for the day*
> *The sticky self that clings*
> *Adhesions on the wings.*
> *To love and adventure*
> *To go on the grand tour*
> *A man must be free*
> *From self-necessity.*

The notion of our *'sticky-self'* clinging to or forming adhesions on the wings of love and adventure is an amazing metaphor. We have to experience this letting go, a dying, in order to go on the grand tour that is our meditation practice.

The poem I wrote below reflects on letting go, about softening, about not being afraid to die daily in the silence of our sitting.

Soften the Edges

> Soften the edges,
> let the boundaries lose their form;
> Don't be afraid of letting go,
> to shape your self into a
> joyful smile...
>
> For are you not just
> a drop of spray
> of the crashing wave

that pounds the shore of
a windswept tide?

Yet, were you, the smallest of drops,
to be cupped gently in our hands,
Would we not, in you, oh little one, see
the entire ocean in all its fullness
and find in you, precious one
in the Oneness of the Tides?

Water is often used to describe the inner condition of those who regularly practice meditation. Jesus speaks of living water, rising up from within. The idea is that, in the silence of our meditation, a spring is opened from within, deep down, and upwards begins to bubble the sacred waters – washing away the sticky-self that adheres to our wings, preventing us from flying free. I wondered what it would be like to be overflowing with such water – or to be as water? I found myself reflecting on this metaphor and wrote this simple poem…

To Be As Water

I hear the call to become as water
for the solid-self
to lose
its sense of substance, shape and size.

I feel the joy of becoming water
no excluding boundaries
no hardness here
no me at all that longs to be
no solidity
when I'm the water.

To soften the edges or to be as water, something needs to give way. We need to lose the sense of our own substance, shape and size to arrive at that place where no hardness remains. Sometimes this softening or washing happens at the most amazing times and in the most simple yet profound ways.

Once, for example, after a yoga class conducted by a particularly compassionate teacher, I was moved to tears. During the movements or *asanas*, it seemed as though a huge pool of ache had been plumbed and opened. Then, as we ended the class with *savasana* (the final resting pose), out poured the grief that had been locked in my body – for how long?

After Yoga

Gently my defences
falling, working on our mats

Slowly the *asanas*
shaping, opening me within
Quietly tears arising
after years of hiding
in my body

In the yoga class
she guides with such grace.

Has it happened to you?

Whispering in the Desert of Love

One of the best books that I have read on grief and trauma is Bessel van der Kolk's *The Body Keeps the Score*. The grief of our traumatic experiences doesn't simply go away or evaporate. Unless we face it and do the grief-work, our body will indeed keep the score.

Meditation is an aid in the healing process. If one's grief or trauma is overwhelming, then clearly additional help is advised in the form of a wise counsellor or therapist. The rhythms of a meditation practice, however, will enable you to access buried feelings and hidden emotional aches – the residues of old wounds. In what Thomas Keating calls 'Divine Therapy', meditation enables us to release the pent-up, unhelpful and possibly toxic emotion, and to let it go. Reading about Keating's understanding of 'Divine Therapy' is highly recommended.

This experience of inner turmoil can be scary. There are times when facing our shadow side is frightening and we may lose our bearings. This is when we need to listen very intentionally in the silence for the whispers of hope that will emerge.

One morning at the Kurisumala Monastery (which I described in an earlier chapter) I sat for several hours at the graveside of the ashram's beloved founder, Francis Acharya. Francis was a Belgian-born Cistercian monk who gave himself to a life of prayerful silence in the hills of Vagamon. Among the many wonderful words he left his brothers were *'listen to the Whispering and whisper to the Listening'*. Putting this into practice is a lifelong balm when gripped by inner fears. The whispering will turn our fears into tears which, when released, usher in the peace we're needing.

■ ■ ■

The Turning

You are the longing and the leaving
the holding on and the letting go
You're the sensual glance, the desiring
the mirrored love, oft weeping
You are the body, aching to be touched
You are your thoughts, flowing without form
You're your soul observing all
You're the passion and the passion's whim
You're every piece and part of this and none of it.
And even when it ends
You'll be a stranger and your only friend.

So wait, hold it all even as it burns,
For as the wheel turns,
so the light follows darkness and
as softness follows hardness
The springtime shall arrive
and you shall survive ...

International spiritual teacher and author, Mirabai Starr, sums it up in her inimitable way in the introduction to the book *Dark Night of the Soul* by John of the Cross: *'God will whisper to the soul in the depth of darkness and guide it through the wilderness of the Unknown until it is annihilated in the flames of perfect love.'*

So fear not – don't be afraid.

A Flame in the Field

As our meditation practice grows, deepens, heals us, freeing us from old wounds it delivers us into a field of wholeness. I've used this phrase – *'the field of wholeness'* – on many occasions to describe, figuratively, what we may experience when meditating.

With practice and intentionality, it is my experience that, in the silence – when I'm sitting still, with my back straight, my heart open and vulnerable, my mind occupied with the saying of my gentle mantra, my attention upon my breath moving in and out – I come upon what feels like a clearing, an open space in the forest of my being. I know that I am in the field of wholeness in the presence of the Other, where no words need to be shared; where in the silence there is comfort, companionship and compassion enough for the entire universe.

In the Upanishads, there is a beautiful verse that suggests that in *'the deepest place of the heart, there is a flame, the size of a thumb; and in that tiny space, are all the worlds, the whole universe, everything that is'*. By adding the image of the flame, we could say that during the stillness of meditation, we may arrive in the field of wholeness and, there in the clearing, draw near to the flame, the size of a thumb in which lives the whole universe, there is everything that is.

Also growing in the field of wholeness are all manner of fruits. These are the fruits of meditation (or of the Spirit, the Christians say) that come alive in us without our knowing, without our trying: equanimity, compassion, wisdom, joy, peace, harmony, insight, patience, goodness, self-understanding, self-control, a longing for justice, a desire for reconciliation…

And thus the awakened ones becomes more fully human, more fully ourselves, more other-centred, and more earth-connected.

As Richard Rohr writes in one of his 'Daily Meditations':

> *Once we experience such intimacy, only the intimate language of lovers describes the experience for us: mystery, tenderness, singularity, specialness, changing the rules 'for me', nakedness, risk, ecstasy, incessant longing…*

And William Butler Yeats sums it up like this:

> *We can make our minds*
> *so like still water*
> *that beings gather about us*
> *that they may see,*
> *it may be, their own images,*
> *and live for a moment with a clearer,*
> *perhaps even with a fiercer life*
> *because of our quiet,*
> *our silence.*

I can't think of anything more meaningful or more purposeful than becoming the still water in which others, even if just for a moment, could see their own images and live, perhaps, a clearer, fiercer life. And so, our wrestling in the Desert of Love is not in vain, nor is it vanity. It's quite the contrary: if we each say 'yes', everything could indeed be born through us.

I once had a sense of this *everything* being *born through me…*

▪ ▪ ▪

Everything Could Be Born Through Me

Spent a day on a river once,
fish eagles overhead,
rhinos grazing nearby,
a fork-tailed drongo chasing the loeries, and
the wind breathing me alive, with
everything being just what it is;

And it reminded me of what
I once had heard, that
Saying 'yes' means to surrender; means
not wanting to possess destiny; and that
that simple word
contains the whole of life!
And if I too could but say it, could
say 'yes' to existence with a total heart, then
everything that should be,
would be
born through me.

Epilogue

The journey is profoundly personal – one that only you can undertake and for which you have only one life, one opportunity. Yet it is beautifully communal; it is a journey that will take us, as Thích Nhất Hạnh says, from our cushion into the community. Meditation isn't simply about saving your own life – it is a commitment to saving the world. Meditation has saved my life, deepened my self-understanding and self-knowledge, and enabled my self-giving and self-surrendering to something bigger than my puny sticky-self.

Developing a meditation practice, embarking on the journey in the Desert of Love, unwrapping ego, finding healing in the clearing light, becoming one with all – this is my real vocation, one much deeper than the priestly call I heard at the age of nine. To end, I don't recall where I heard this story, but it serves to remind us of a marvellous truth as we journey in the Desert of Love...

> *A disciple once asked a very wise and spiritual teacher or shaman the question, 'How can I be more like you?' The teacher paused, smiled gently and replied, 'If you want to be more like me, be more like yourself.' He was teaching that the road to spiritual fulfilment – or what in some traditions is called enlightenment – is paved with authenticity, not imitation. Here is a parable or allegory to illustrate:*
>
> *There once was an African elder who loved to meditate on a favourite rock alongside the river. He would go there daily, early in the morning, and embrace the quiet while the river slowly washed past. Sometimes he would enjoy some fruit depending on the season.*
>
> *One day, quite suddenly and without warning, while he was savouring a tasty avocado and reflecting on the wonder of God, a shaft of bright light broke through the leaves above him. In a flash he realised he was one with all life, eternally whole, and filled with grace and peace. After some while, he realised that he had had a profound encounter with God.*
>
> *Later, when he returned to the village, everyone realised there was something extraordinary about him; he had been transformed and glowed with a new light. When the villagers asked,*

'What happened to you?', he explained: 'I was just sitting on the big rock down by the river, eating an avocado, when a bright beam of light fell upon me and I encountered God.'

The next morning when he awoke, there was no one in the village. He looked in all the huts, but everyone had mysteriously disappeared. After some time, he decided to give up searching and return, as was his practice, to the rock at the river on which he loved to sit.

When he arrived, he was amazed to find all the people from the village clustered around the rock, avocados in hand, scrambling to get to the top.

The wise elder laughed and went off to find himself another quiet place, where maybe God would visit again.

So, let's go find *our* rock!

Sadhu, May I Walk With You?

Embracing the path of emptiness

■ ■ ■

ONCE UPON A TIME in India, there lived a boy who was dearly loved by his mother and father. One day, while playing in the garden, he was bitten by a poisonous snake. His horrified parents, aware that their son's life was at risk, and that the only hospital in the region was several days drive away, rushed him to a holy man who lived in a cave in the mountains. The holy man said he wasn't sure if he could do anything, but that they could try an ancient ritual in the hope that it would heal the boy. The holy man explained that the ritual required all involved to confess their sins and account for any wrongdoings. Anxiously, they all agreed to this condition.

So, the holy man put his hand on the boy's head and confessed his sins, saying that he wasn't as holy as everyone thought; that he sometimes neglected his prayers and sometimes ate meat, and didn't fast as much as he should. Having accounted for all his sins, *and openly and honestly recommitted himself to a life of holiness, they noticed that the boy opened his eyes. But he wasn't able to talk or move.*

So, the boy's father came forward and putting his hand on the boy's heart, confessed, saying how often he had put money making first and his marriage and family second, and how his greed and avarice governed his life. He committed to amend his ways and, as he thus confessed, the boy sat up, smiled at them, but remained unable to talk.

So, the boy's mother came forward and, putting her fingers on the boy's lips, she confessed her sins, saying how often she had allowed anger, pride and envy to poison her relationships, and how self-centred her life had become.

Having confessed and promised to amend her ways, the boy opened his mouth and was able to address them: 'Thank you, holy man, father and mother for your honest confessions, for it was revealed to me that only by your truthfulness was it possible for me to be healed. But wait! More was revealed to me, while I lay dying.'

'Tell us, please, dear son,' the adults said anxiously. 'What more was revealed to you?'

So, speaking slowly and thoughtfully, the boy began:

'It was revealed to me that each of you awaits your true vocation, your awakening, your calling, for how you are living now is but a half- life.

You're asleep in your minds, your hearts are closed, your lives are slipping away, and your future is heavy with suffering unless you awaken.'

'Help us, please!' cried the adults. 'What must we do?'

'Awaken today to your heart's true desire. Wash the sleep from your eyes and look within. There, a path awaits. Follow it, without looking back,' said the boy.

Many years later, in the region where the boy lived, a magnificent transformation had taken place. A holy man had become the abbot of a nearby monastery in which many miracles of healing were said to occur in any who spent time there in prayer.

Of equal interest was that a very successful and wealthy businessman had sold his businesses and become a dedicated and generous community leader, working alongside all in the community to build schools, clinics, farms, roads, and all manner of significant and lasting projects bringing justice and peace to the region.

Apparently, too, there was a mother from that region who returned to school and, after graduating, became first the mayor of the town, then governor of the region. Many thought it was only a matter of time before she became the first woman prime minister of the whole of India.

But the people of the region always loved to tell of the little boy who had lived amongst them – whose joy was infectious, whose wisdom was beyond his years, and whose heart was so full of love that all wept when he hugged them. They told, too, of the day he fell ill again, this time with a sickness for which there was no known cure, and how, as he lay dying, he had addressed them:

'Dear friends ... Don't mourn my dying, don't cry for me. Not only have I seen what awaits us, but I am also among the most blessed, knowing that my vocation, my task in life, my work and purpose has been accomplished. And though I die, I live on. Weep rather for those who are dead, even though they live.'

※ ※ ※

I first heard this story a long time ago and, when trying to recall it, I couldn't accurately remember how it ended, so I crafted an ending that makes the point of the story clear, if not elemental. We are not alive until we awaken. Consciousness is the road home. There may be many aha moments, or our awakening may be the consequence of an unwelcome body blow – the death of a loved one, the diagnosis of a serious condition – but awaken we must. To live consciously is to be both fully human and fully divine. For believers in God, one truth should constantly enliven our minds and hearts. It's of a Source of Love constantly wooing us, collectively and personally, deeply desiring our awakening. A God of Love is, by definition, a calling-God, a waiting-God, a desperately hoping-God, a longing-God – one whose joy is fulfilled when we are awakened and when we begin to live in the reality beyond the veil.

To Awaken

To awaken;
To smell the aroma of the real Presence in every daily round,
To see in every sunset, the Heart of fire
To hear in every whisper, a sacred invitation
To taste, with my whole being, the Spirit's sacred fruits,
With every touch, to pull aside a veil and enter in,
And there to awaken to the
one Original Face, and
know it to be both God's and mine

To Awaken

Retirement: Leaving the Organisation, Not the Journey

As I entered my sixties, I found myself less concerned with the form and shape of the church to which I had belonged for so many years. More important was its impact – its need to break down the walls of resistance and become the community of love envisaged by its founder. Less important were the rules and dogmas, and more important was the longing to be an inclusive and non-judgmental family venturing beyond the veil, discovering the meeting place within where God and humanity are One.

This was my prayer, my desire and my experience…

On turning 60

After walking the long-looking paths,
my journey turning, at last
inward and to whole-making,
takes me, with all my resisting
for fear of being exposed, beyond
ego's glittering
but lifeless tomb
my feigning face all this time
thought was home; and
from which, as I surrender and awaken
to the real journey, I find
my sacred truer-self walking freely
the deep and joyful trail
of my true design.

I felt I had walked many long-looking paths and yet I was about to begin a new journey, one beyond *'ego's glittering but lifeless tomb'* that for so long I had called home. As I surrendered and let go of my ambitions and organisational attachments, I felt my *'sacred truer-self walking freely the deep and joyful trail of my true design'*.

Letting go is an essential part of growth. My longing for visibility, recognition and appreciation was diminishing. Ego's glittering desire for status was a tomb-like shadow – an illusion. This realisation was due, in large part, to the power of stillness – the experience of God discovered within a regular practice of silence, of meditation. In my opinion, the life-giving word of God is usually heard as inaudible whispers that come to us in the sheer silence, just as Elijah discovered in the cave. *'Be still and know that I am God'* says the psalmist.

It's within our ability to be still, and what happens in the stillness is up to God, but it is always life-giving and transformative.

For those who believe in the Easter story as a central metaphor for our lives, I wrote a brief poem reflecting my awakening to the true status to which I was being called, and to which everyone is called. The status I longed for wasn't to be bestowed on me by the church. Rather, it was the status I discovered as I died to my ego's longings and desires – of being set free to walk not *behind*, but *alongside* God.

Easter Understanding

Each Easter, dear One, I come
to understand anew
that your call to me 'arise and walk' means
no longer behind, but alongside you;
Not embalmed in self's small tomb;
But with uncovered face, set free
from the me

that died, with you
on Friday afternoon.

Since retiring I have been asked (as is every retiree, I imagine) what retirement is like? My answer increasingly reflects the realisation that it is only the organisation from which one retires. My need to belong is increasingly not wrapped up with an organisation. I feel as though I belong to something larger, the wider family of sojourners, the family of those on the journey of life. There is no retiring from this journey. Not that it is easy, this belonging to something larger! I frequently feel the pain of my old wounds, my inner demons, but in truth they haunt me less – just sometimes and still with distress. But the wounds and demons are not the true-me, and I need not fear their random visits. We come to learn that much of the light creeps in through these wounds, and we may even become thankful for them.

To wear my wound as a badge of honour

To wear my wound as a badge of honour,
To accept its offering, let it sing
To live in the narrowing of shadows,
while edging into the light,
nursed by Love's delight.
Though darkness may rise within me
I'll wear my wound as a badge of honour,
tonight.

The Mother who is India

For several years, Jacqui and I have had the opportunity to travel fairly widely in India. Visiting India was a goal, a dream of Jacqui's, and I am deeply grateful for her determination to save for and plan our visits to what acclaimed travel writer, William Dalrymple, called the last truly spiritual society left in the world. While the modernisation of India is breath-taking, the changes to the fabric of this ancient world are irreversible and, in many cases, worrying. The dominant extract-manufacture-consume-discard model of western capitalism has entrenched itself in India. Yroups of the religious run into the millions. Within these groups, notwithstanding the dominance of Hinduism, some practise faith-based rituals that reach deep into the Indian psyche. One can't spend any decent length of time there and come away unchanged – well, that's been my experience.

In India, it feels to me that the glorious trichotomy of body, mind and spirit is fully present and celebrated, whereas we westerners live in a dichotomous world of mind and body. Walking down a street in India is to be washed through in body, mind and spirit. Everything is alive and every sense is overwhelmed by the sheer opulence of the experience.

Our travels around India have shaped my later years in a very significant way. I have struggled to write something substantial about this, although I have written smaller pieces in other parts of this anthology, but here's what has always felt to me like an unfinished poem, seeking to express some thoughts about this majestic Mother and her unique calling to each of us...

Our Mother India

An ancient face etched with selfless lines
eyes as purple pools of time, call to each of us, who
reach like infants for her stirring breast,
feeling life arise with each primordial breath, that
gently presses past her purséd lips,
inviting us to pause our puny monkey-minds,
and hear a Mother's sigh,

'Come drink the ancient silence
found by those who make their home in me.'

But will you know me, I cautiously ask of her,
for there are so many like me –
a tailor sewing saffron cloth,
a trader sorting cumin spice,
a Dalit sweeping with handmade broom;
a barber with blade on client's face,
a bus driver seeking fares from those upstairs;
a merchant hanging sarees, near the wallahs selling chai,
while mothers say good-bye to scholars on a tram,
with tuk-tuks darting, a tourist bargaining,
each one making their home in you?

Can I trust you, again I ask this ancient One
with her spice-rich spirit, all bright red and gold, and
a million portraits young and old; a billion stories being told;
Is mine amongst them, Mother, do you see me, in such diversity?
Can I be known in such a sea of humanity?
Can I trust beyond my fear, amidst the noise and pain
of countless others, all of whom wait to hear
their precious names being called by you?

O Great Mother, you hear my heart's clear cry,
Remind me why, I should have no fear?
That it is your timeless pulse beating here, in me
an ancient reflection of our primeval unity;
Retell of the time, as life began,
when all was One, and since then
you've known the name of everyone
gone before and still to come; and
Remind me dear Mother

of the promise you've made to all humanity
that compassionately, you'll call us to return and
with unprotected hearts,
we'll hear your sacred promising, whispering
'Come, come drink the ancient silence;
come, make your home in me.'

Of Forest Dwellers and Sadhus

In Hindu tradition and mythology there are four life stages known as *ashramas*. First there is *brahmacharya* or student stage; second, *grihastha,* the householder stage; then *vanaprastha,* the forest dweller. Most don't get beyond this third stage, but there is a fourth stage – that of the male *sadhu* or female *sadhvi*, which describes one who is an ascetic wanderer.

The Bhagavad Gita says of the *sadhu* and *sadhvi* that they are the ones *who do not hate, do not desire, and are without dualities; truly, they are liberated from bondage.* These noteworthy people embrace a form of asceticism marked by the renunciation of material desires and longings. They live in a state of detachment from ordinary daily life, with the purpose of spending time in peaceful, love-inspired, simple spiritual life. These Hindu ascetics have their sisters and brothers in other great faiths, such as the *bhikkhus and bhikkhunīs* of Buddhism and the monks and nuns of Christianity.

In Hindu terms, I would be considered a forest dweller. Having sold our family home and packed up what is left of our belongings in preparation to travel Asia for an unspecified time, it feels very much as though I have graduated from the householder stage. Being a forest dweller conjures a host of images: the forest is a place of exploration, of intrigue, of discovery, and even of disappearing. The forest is, at least to me, a place of shadows – a Jungian's delight.

Throughout life we stuff our unwanted and scary feelings, emotions, memories and experiences into the shadows. This is the stage to explore them, expose them, delve into them, and bring them into the healing light.

From a spiritual perspective, the forest motif brings to mind gentle paths leading to clearings in the woods where one can pause and recollect. In some meditation teachings, the terms 'clearing' is used to describe the gap between our tumbling thoughts, when the mind is stilled sufficiently that there appears to be a pause or gap between thoughts. In this gap, between the thoughts, lie the rich pickings of presence. This is the meeting place where the Other and the true-self discover their conjoint identity. This is the home of cosmic consciousness, the origin of Love, our glimpse of the Great Explosion (what science calls the Big Bang).

It is the forest dweller's great joy to play in the clearing – to delve into the mystery of life and love, to be drawn by the Source into a deeper relationship with love. The forest dweller falls into the consciousness that what is at play here, in the forest, is not a Christian love story, but a cosmic love story in which everyone and everything is embraced and included. So much has been beautifully written about this love so generously shared by the Source of Love with we who are the prime partners in the love story.

Such beautiful art – poetry, sonnets and prose – seeks to describe it, like this stanza from Rumi:

> *In your light, I learn how to love*
> *In your beauty, how to make poems*
> *You dance inside my chest*
> *where no one sees you*
> *But sometimes I do*
> *and that sight*
> *becomes this art.*

Here is my attempt at capturing my experience of this wondrous and mystical love…

A Taste of Love

My heart, a spray of waves,
upon the shore, wanting more;
Your breath along my spine,
a moving tide of tenderness,
a rising sacredness, set free;
Your tenderness, a rising sun, o'er the sea,
all gold and red;
Nothing said, but 'Yes'
yes to you, my Lord,
my taste of love.

And another reflection on this mystery – a journal entry titled 'Flowing like a river without diminishing', which I wrote after a morning meditation:

Today – just sitting in the glow of meditation-peace and a deep appreciation for the growing coming together (integration) of the wild parts of me … I can trust I'm on the path … a real experience of joy and excitement at the homecoming and inclusion of the many prodigal pieces of me … Though I'm uncertain as to where it will all lead, I trust the path and the One guiding me … Then, I recall words from Sarah Blondin, the leader of a ten-day online course I've just completed, called 'My Deepest Self', in which she describes a place deep within us – a neutral place (the clearing?) of solid ground not tossed and shaken by mood or thought or emotion or orientation …our true home … to which we can go at any time and where we always find the peace born of the intrinsic nature of the place itself – a place not governed by our common constructs, such as Jew or Gentile, straight or gay, male or female, slave or free … It is the space of truth beyond categories and constructs … accepting, non-judging and welcoming – it is Love's abode … the Shepherd's Hut … It is within, everywhere, and it is nowhere … such joy is this mysteriousness!

Irina Tweedie (1907–1999), a very dear Sufi teacher, once explained:

> *There are moments of oneness with the Beloved, absolute ecstasy and bliss. That is nothingness. And this nothingness loves you, responds to you, fulfils you utterly and yet there is nothing there.*
> *You flow out like a river without diminishing. This is the great mystical experience, the great ecstasy…*

Every Day an Embrace

We can see and embrace, this love every day. All around us are signs of love, messages of hope and promises of companionship.

For example, on my birthday this year (2021), in the exquisite fynbos garden I discovered Love's presence all atwitter and all around …

It was a magnificent February morning. Our rented cottage shares one of False Bay's most enthralling gardens, tenderly created by and cared for by our landlords (we prefer the term *land-people*) Kate and Geoff. Backing onto the mountain, paths meander up steps through the fynbos.

Here you can sit for hours watching the changing faces of nature throughout the year. Or, if you prefer, you can watch the surf below. It's a place of real splendour.

Arriving in the Garden
(A birthday poem)

Arriving in the garden on this clear-eyed morning
She offers herself to me,
opening her dewy secrets unhesitatingly…
Two sunbirds flit a whimsy welcome,
their red-winged starling sisters
on gentle breezes arising from the
tumbling ancient tides below,
whose waves unfold their foamy selves
upon the rocky shelves of our ancestral shore,

while, alongside, twelve March lilies, blooming just for me,
in February! (or so it seems)
eagerly stretch their flimsy stems
towards the rising sun
whose caress upon the eastern clouds
is but a burnished trim,
announcing the arriving
of another royal dawning
of her ageless gift of day-hood
of which I've had my long and lucky share
Each of which has been,
as is this today,
a birthday gift of grace to me.

Arriving in the Garden

This next poem was inspired by a taxi speeding past me, my eye catching words written above the windscreen in isiXhosa, which became my mantra the following morning as I sat in meditation…

uYesu ulungile

Splashed on the speeding taxi passing by
I read the words
uYesu ulungile,
and take them as a mantra
for my time of prayer today; and so
with single-pointed breath
and settling mind,
I let their gentle sound
carry me away…
uYesu ulungile
uYesu ulungile
uYesu ulungile…
Until I hear the chime
that ends my morning time of prayer.
And rising up, I'm thankful for
the way the taxi's passing by
has shaped my day
and commit myself to be the one
to share with those I pass…
uYesu ulungile,
Jesus is good.

uYesu uLingile

Finally, this little piece of sweet theology, made more real this year living alongside the spangled waters of False Bay, filled with its ceaseless swells and crashing waves...

Love is the Sea

As God is love,
So is love the sea and we, the fish
moving, breathing, our being filled,
surrendered to the sea
in which there is life and love
enough for all.

Love is the Sea

On the Path of Emptiness

In the Christian tradition, there is a wonderful but sadly underemphasised piece of theology referred to as 'kenosis'. Essentially kenosis means 'the act of emptying', and refers to the self-emptying of Jesus in form but not in nature when, as Christians believe, Jesus became human and lived as a servant and willing participant in the human drama of vulnerability, suffering and death.

This isn't the place for a detailed explanation or exegesis of the passages supporting this doctrine, especially as taught by St Paul in the letter to the Philippians. Rather, let's simply recognise that for Jesus, this self-emptying was a significant thing – something he modelled and taught. Just as he emptied himself, becoming a humble servant to humankind; just as he continually chose the lesser way, the way of forgiveness, the path of non-violence, the way of turning the other cheek, the way of non-materialism; and just as he chose the side of the outcast, the poor, those on the edge – so he taught that we should do the same. It is in dying that we find life. If we want to follow his way, we need to take up our cross and follow him, which is to say that dying is required in order to be a follower. The central pillar of his teaching and modelling, his core conviction, was that love is stronger than death, and that the laying down of self, which is the essence of this love, leads not to death, but to life!

All this points to the highly counter-intuitive notion found in many faiths that, ironically, in order to fully live a life of meaning and purpose, we need to lay something down, let something go, die to that which keeps us captive, which is our grasping and defending egoic self – that false-self or clay wrapping that covers our true-self, the golden Buddha or Christ-nature within.

In the Lord's Prayer, the phrase *'Your will be done'* gets to the point of the matter: not *my will* but *yours*. Surrendering to a will other than one's own is the basis of every confession of faith throughout the world's faiths. Surrender is the gatepost to the field of wholeness. There is no alternative entrance.

In some Christian circles, and especially in the monastic tradition, this surrendering was known as *the path of descent* and was evident in someone's life by their actions. The primary action was to walk down the path of no belongings – choosing poverty.

Another was the letting go of sexual relationships – choosing celibacy. A third was the surrendering of one's will to that of a guide, mentor or spiritual community – choosing the way of obedience.

Choosing a life of poverty, celibacy and obedience was an eminently *kenotic way of living* and a very clear indication of one's commitment to following Jesus' way and teaching. Not everyone need follow this way, but all may choose to *honour the intent of this way* by being less materialistic, living reverent lives (especially with those with whom we share sexual intimacy), and by being willing to live a more community-centred life, honouring the needs of others over our own..

In Hinduism, the *sadhus* and *sadhvis* are very clearly on this path. Having given up all material belongings, embracing celibacy and living simply according to the principles of their faith, they begin the journey on the path of descent. Figuratively speaking, every *sadhu* and *sadhvi* is journeying to the beatific city of Varanasi, where every pious Hindu hopes to die and be cremated on the great Ghats of the Sacred Ganges on which their ashes may set sail for Nirvana.

What has all of this to do with me? Well, in truth, like many others, I have always felt called to walk the path of descent. Were it not for my very happy and blessed marriage to Jacqui, I could indeed have joined a religious order, become a monk. I've always aspired to simplicity, to the letting go of encumbrances, of living closer to the earth, being less occupied with the comforts that Joel McKerrow calls the empire's *'far-reaching … programmes of consumer sedation, killing the imagination'* in his poem *'The Wild Ones'*. The truth is that Jacqui is the most unmaterialistic person I know – far more so than me and it is she who has motivated us to simplify and live more intentionally. It was she who encouraged me to embrace vegetarianism. It was she who taught me to put savings into travel and not things. She's thoroughly anti-empire and resists far better than I the programmes of consumer sedation so abundant in our world today.

And so, very aware that I haven't yet fully completed my forest dweller stage, the time has come and a window of opportunity has opened for us to embrace a more kenotic way of being – or to put it figuratively, to embark on the way of the *sadhu* and *sadhvi*.

Although we are about to embark on a real journey and live nomadically in Southeast Asia, we're also starting a deeper spiritual journey.

We seek to venture down all sorts of paths – into meditation halls, yoga studios, ashrams and market places, forests and other places yet unknown and maybe, who knows, we will one day arrive at Varanasi where our egos can find their pyres and turn to dust, setting us free to sail further down the Great Ganges of life's adventures!

But whatever occurs in the ensuing years, this is for me a deeply spiritual thing. I really do want to walk *the paths of descent* and find that place where we *become ourselves, surrendered and free to love, to watch and wait…*

In many respects, this poem is my mantra for the next years. I pray I'll be faithful to it…

There I Must Go

I choose to take the path of descent
and seek at last, my name;
not the name I've sought so hard to make;
not the name I've wanted them to know;
but the name I heard in the womb;
the name of my soul.
For there, in lowly places,
like wombs and mangers,
at workbenches and around old kitchen tables,
there we become ourselves;
and there,
surrendered and free to live and love,
to watch and wait,
there, I must go, I choose to go…

And here, two poems reflecting my statement of commitment to the end-point:

To End in Emptiness

Surrendered but noble,
this soul,
her chosen goal,
to end in emptiness.

No fear or fight;
no struggle to become;
In light, at night,
she courses her path,
gliding, glistening, guided by
a sacred, primal pulse
unheld and unaware,
unlike this anxious thinking-me.

Mindful she flows, with
no thought of self;
Caressing all she touches
with moistened lips,
in undiscovered ravines
deep within my heart, from
where she arises
each new day,
carrying me with her
in this third age of mine.

Sadhu, may I walk with you?

The Contemplative's Way

I came upon a holy man and asked him
'Sir, what are you doing?'
'Nothing,' he answered
'And Sir,' I asked, 'where are you going?'
'Nowhere,' he said.
And I knew at last
I had found one I could follow.
So I followed
And found his path was long
and his work was hard.

And finally, a poem not unlike those above, that is really a prayer – an asking, in a sense – that I may be found worthy (as the prophet Micah suggested, a thousand years ago) to walk humbly, to act justly and to love compassionately!

Sadhu, May I Walk with You?

Sadhu, may I walk with you
on your way to Varanasi?
May I suffer, too
as do you
and awaken in me
a heart wide enough to
save tonight
all, who out of sight
die alone
in homes unknown

What Shall We Say About Love?

I want to end this chapter and anthology with a joyful piece on love. A dear friend, Herschelle, who had been in a long relationship with her partner, Ricado, was to be married! Alleluia, we all sang! Joy upon happiness. Grace upon grace! Confirmation of commitment. A new chapter in their lives. A public declaration of a private union. Naturally, I was delighted to be asked to conduct much of the ceremony and, especially for Herschelle and Ricado, I composed this narrative, adapted from the writings of Kahlil Gibran and Paul of Tarsus.

Reflection on Love

Narrator: *What shall we say about love? How shall we describe its origin or its workings? How can we summon it to come upon those we love – that their love for each other may be strengthened and endure the struggles of life? For of this we are certain. Love is our purpose, our meaning, our heart's deepest desire. And without it, our lives are but dust, fragments blown apart by the winds of circumstance.*

Voice 1: *If I have great eloquence, or the gift of oratory, but do not have love, I am only a resounding gong or a clanging cymbal. If I have great vision and can inspire people to believe in a future for all, or if I acquire great knowledge and can discern the mysteries of life, or if I have the kind of belief to move the mountains of poverty, injustice, inequality, but do not have love, I am nothing.*

Voice 2: *Even if I surrender my life and all I own to live alongside the poorest of the poor, but do not have love, it will not benefit anyone. For love is source of all life. From love we come and into love we shall dissolve at the end. Love alone gives meaning to life. Love is our deepest desire, our highest aspiration.*

Narrator: *And what shall it be like to know this love? To be summoned by it? To be love's companion?*

Voice 3: *When love beckons you, follow love's lead, even though love's ways may be hard and steep. And when love's wings enfold you, yield within them, even though the sword hidden among the pinions may from time to time wound you. And when love speaks to you, believe the voice you are hearing, even though love may shatter your dreams as the north wind lays waste the garden. For love is for your growth and for your pruning. And just as love ascends to your height and caresses your most tender branches quivering in the sun, so shall love descend to your roots and shake them in their clinging to the earth. For love knows you from the beginning and knows of what you are made, and what beauty and goodness lies within you.*

Voice 1: *And so, love will gather you as the worker of the land gathers sheaves of corn, and by threshing and sifting them frees them from the husks that hide the fruit within. So you too will be gathered and sifted, that your true beauty and goodness may be revealed. And even thereafter, love will assign you to the sacred fire, that you may become sacred bread for God's sacred feast. All these things shall love do unto you that you may know the secrets of your heart, and in that knowledge become a part of Love's great heart.*

Narrator: *And how shall we know that what we feel is love and not something pretending to be love? What is the true nature of love? How can we describe it?*

Voice 2: *Love is patient, love is kind. It does not envy, it does not boast, it is not proud. It does not dishonour others, it is not self-seeking, it is not easily angered, it keeps no record of wrongs. Love does not delight in evil but rejoices in the truth. It always protects, always trusts, always hopes, always perseveres. Love never fails.*

Narrator: *And will love really be ours to possess?*

Voice 3: *When you love you should not say, 'God is in my heart', but rather, 'I am in the heart of God'. For love is God's gift to you – though it be your birth right, for every child of God receives every gift God has to give, without discrimination. But even though love is yours, do* *not possess it or try to own it. Give it away as quickly as you receive it. Let it flow through you, and so become Love's channel, and in your emptiness you shall ever be full.*

Narrator: *And so in the name of this love, we gather today to witness this love; and in the name of love we celebrate and ask that the Source of Love bless us/you. And our prayer is this:*

That you may melt into one and be like a running brook that sings its melody to the night;
That you may know the pain of too much tenderness;
That you may wake at dawn with a winged heart and give thanks for another day of loving;
That you may rest at the noon hour and meditate love's ecstasy;
That you may return home at eventide with gratitude;
And sleep with a prayer for your beloved in your heart and a song of praise upon your lips.
For in the end, only three things shall remain: faith hope and love. But the greatest of these is love. Amen

Lee's Farewell

LEE RICHARD COLTHAM
(26 July 1974 – 30 August 2021)

■ ■ ■

I'm sitting at my desk composing this anthology. My phone displays an incoming call from Barry Coltham, a friend of over 60 years, but he's in Tanzania enjoying Ngorongoro and beyond. Over the many years we have witnessed myriad experiences that have deepened and cemented our friendship. Motorbikes, girlfriends, marriages, the birth of children, the death of parents, homes, holidays and so much more. His voice is urgent. It's about his first-born, Lee, my very beloved godson. 'We think Lee has had a heart attack,' he says. I rush to the house, arriving as the paramedic declares Lee's time of death. Nothing could be done. Everything has come undone. Lee is dead. We are in shock. This is not possible. Never. One so full of life, filled with such talent, with such abundance and energy, with such passion for living, on whom so many depend, in the prime of his life, just as the fruits of enormous effort were beginning to flower, is gone. The one who burst into life, was always bursting into new chapters and ventures, has left us. We weep even though we know life is impermanent and that, like the grass of the field, we blossom one day, then the wind blows and our place is no more. Love indeed breaks us open. And as so many parents know only too well, parents shouldn't be burying their children. Days later at alongside our favourite Langebaan Lagoon, his special place, we commemorated his life with song, poems, prayers and tributes.

Lee's Farewell

Lee's Farewell

My godson died today

Too young, too soon, so much more to give,
to know, to show the ones he loved, and
to be loved by the ones he's left, bereft, behind.

But I shouldn't say, hey Lee?
that you were '*my* godson'
For you belonged to everyone,
you were *our son*, the one
we knew from the day
you burst into our world
so naive then, 47 years ago…

Who would know we'd be here today
sharing this grief, your life too brief,
Struggling to find the words to say goodbye
and why,
why must you leave us now
and how,
how shall we live without your
endless energy,
your generous giving,
your big-hearted loving
Your joyful 'do-it-my-way' way of living?

And how we loved you then,
immediately, at first sight
without a doubt,
that first night of
June 26, 1974, when you arrived saying

This is me!
Lee Richard Coltham, *actually*!
And made yourself at home,
in Gran-gran's house and in our hearts,
where you showed us, no,
from the start, you *told* us
how to raise a child … just a little wild
And no thank you, you'd say,
I won't blow my nose today
or change my clothes today,
for as far I can see
Everyone loves me
even when I'm running around naked.

And love you, we did
and have since then
Lee Richard Coltham,
throughout the years,
watching you discover who you really are,
and who you'd like to be…
Sometimes afar, sometimes near, the fear
that you would lose your way
was never ours.
And even now
we know you'll make a path of light
beyond the night
that's enveloped us.

And, if we listen carefully, we'll hear you calling
Follow me, you'll see, it'll turn out beautifully.

For you've always been one
for making paths and plans and lists

Endless lists, so that nothing would be missed
Especially if it involved having fun
An opportunity for all to see
how good they looked wearing
pink or green as long as it meant
bursting into song,
and other people's photographs
for a laugh, late into the night.

But always there was time to pause
especially for those of yours –
your beautiful and beloved ones
the children of your delight.
For you were a child's Dad –
your love for them undiminished,
undeterred, always present
holding, guiding,
filling their hearts and minds
with tales of adventure,
Of how much there is to do in life
And that in every day
there should be time to play
something cool,
like only you could do…

Just speaking for myself finally, dear Lee if I may?
Though sometimes life and work and things got in our way
there was not a birthday in forty-seven years
that I missed reminding you (as a godfather has to do)
of the one undisputed truth
buried deep within everyone…

That all of life is a kind of listening,
a kind of learning, an understanding
of the reason that we're here,
the reason for our birth,
the reason for our visit to this earth…
Is to learn about Love
Not some soppy thing from above,
but a visceral, real, human, deep, emotional love,
that lives in the deep-down within;
A love that seeps in
and through our skin even
when our demons come, we learn
that it's Love we can trust,
That's the only gift we've got to give,
Our only lasting offering,
is Love.
It's the only thing that matters,
that really matters.

And looking at your life,
and at your beautiful family,
it seems to me,
you were mastering this gift of love,
Or maybe it was mastering you –
as love tends to do
But either way, we've come today,
this sad, grief-filled day,
this final day come too soon
to entrust you to this Love
so much larger than all of ours combined
a love that each will find and
make our own.

So, into this Love,
this larger, lighter, brighter Love
We entrust you,
we commend you,
we release you,
but never will forget you
Lee Richard Coltham,
beloved one...

Go in peace

A Final Word

For the past year, and while compiling this anthology, Jacqui and I have been living in a cottage owned by a remarkable and ageless couple, Kate and Geoff Davies. Renting their little garden cottage in Kalk Bay has been a magical gift – a delight, a joy. Not only did it provide us with a beautiful temporary home in an exquisite fynbos garden with untiring views over False Bay, but it also provided us with the opportunity to witness a couple for whom the notion of retirement clearly makes no sense. Kate and Geoff are free spirits who delight in the abounding nature around them, but, more importantly, they are environmental justice warriors. Their long history of eco-activism, including the founding of the South African Faith Communities' Environment Institute (SAFCEI) is well known. Geoff, a retired bishop of the Anglican Church, has been known as the 'Green Bishop' for many years. Their commitment to caring for the living Earth comes from a deep place and is lived out in every aspect of their daily lives.

I've been challenged by their faith-based commitment to environmental justice, and have come to see my shortcomings in this regard. While we have been committed to doing our part, to living more simply so that others may simply live, and while my theology embraces a God profoundly engaged in and concerned about every aspect of creation, and while we unquestioningly and regularly add our voices to the demands for environmental justice, I know that there is much more I need to do. And this, for me, is the next frontier. I take to heart Pierre Teilhard de Chardin's powerful and implicit challenge – 'The Age of Nations is past. The task before us now, if we would not perish, is to build the Earth' – made particularly real by the Davies.

As we venture into the unknown future, seeking to live simple nomadic lives, I commit myself to earth building, climate justice and sustainable living as integral dimensions of my daily practice, promising to remain open to the many teachings I have yet to learn in this task before us all.

Richard Rohr recently quoted from a plea issued in 1990 by Indigenous leaders at the Global Forum on Environment and Development for Survival. It provides a clear map for my further exploration:

> *We have jeopardized the future of our coming generation with our greed and lust for power. The warnings are clear and time is now a factor ... We speak of our children, yet we savage the spawning beds of the salmon and herring, and kill the whale in his home. We advance through the forests of the earth, felling our rooted brothers indiscriminately, leaving no seeds for the future. We exploit the land and resources of the poor and indigenous peoples of the world. We have become giants, giants of destruction ... We must return to the spiritual values that are the foundation of life. We must love and respect all living things, have compassion for the poor and the sick, respect and understanding for women and female life on this earth who bear the sacred gift of life. We must return to the prayers, ceremonies, meditations, rituals, and celebrations of thanksgiving, which link us with the spiritual powers that sustain us and, by example, teach our children to respect.*

Finally, I draw inspiration for this work from a litany adapted from Andre Auger's beautiful work:

> *God, you work...*
> *in the accelerating expansion of the universe*

in the spiralling of galaxies
in the explosion of supernovas
in the singularity of black holes
in the regularity of the Solar System
in the equilibrium of the Earth's ecology
in the evolving of a society
in the thoughts of an individual
in corporate and political decisions
in the functioning of our organs
in the chemical processes within our bodies
in the forces within the atom
in the behaviour of quantum particles …
May I sit in wonder that I live entirely within your Presence
everywhere and in everything and everyone. Amen.

With special thanks to my Art Class!

Thanks and Acknowledgements

For the inspiration, encouragement and accompaniment during the past seven years, I wish to thank with all my heart the following beautiful people:

My wife, Jacqui – my rock and most loving, loyal and honest companion on the journey. May our next nomadic chapter together be as amazing!

My daughters Kate and Zoe, for their loving, gentle feedback and support, for their belief in me and, for their unequivocal blessing on their parents' upcoming nomadic adventure.

To the beautiful people of St Margaret's, Parow – my family of the past seven years – for their love and patience, and for listening so willingly to my many poems and reflections. And to the wider family of the Diocese of Saldanha Bay, especially the bishop, for embracing and welcoming me into the diocese.

To Herschelle Milford, for unfailingly providing comment and critique on the poems and illustrations, and for her infectious belief in creativity.

To my dear family and special friends who never seem to mind when I post yet another poem, and for unhesitatingly agreeing to buy the publications.

To Bronwen Dachs Muller and Hilda Hermann for their magnificent editorial work on this manuscript.

To the best art teacher in the world, Sasha Scholtz, and the best Tuesday-morning art class family in the world, whose inspiration and backing has been unbelievably generous. Always in my heart!

And to you, readers of this anthology: thank you, thank you, thank you! May love be yours to give away with complete abandon!

www.ingramcontent.com/pod-product-compliance
Lightning Source LLC
Chambersburg PA
CBHW080409230426
43662CB00016B/2359